THE
PENTAGON
of FAITH

THE PENTAGON of FAITH

SACRED THEISM VS. SECULAR HUMANISM

A Christian's Need for the
Traditional Faith of Our Fathers
(THE FAITH SERIES BOOK 1)

Dr. Donald R. Hayes

DILLON, SOUTH CAROLINA
June 21, 2012

The Pentagon of Faith

Copyright © 2023 by Dr. Donald R. Hayes. All rights reserved.

No part of this publication may be reproduced, stored in a retrieval system or transmitted in any way by any means, electronic, mechanical, photocopy, recording or otherwise without the prior permission of the author except as provided by USA copyright law.

The opinions expressed by the author are not necessarily those of URLink Print and Media.

1603 Capitol Ave., Suite 310 Cheyenne, Wyoming USA 82001
1-888-980-6523 | admin@urlinkpublishing.com

URLink Print and Media is committed to excellence in the publishing industry.

Book design copyright © 2023 by URLink Print and Media. All rights reserved.

Published in the United States of America

Library of Congress Control Number: 2023902791
ISBN 978-1-68486-364-8 (Paperback)
ISBN 978-1-68486-367-9 (Digital)

06.02.23

Dedication

To my wife Cynthia Bush Hayes and Justin White, my 39 year old son-in-law, who died of Covid-19.

'For of Him, and through Him, and to Him, are all things: to whom be glory forever. Amen.'
(KJV) Romans 11:36

Contents

Acknowledgments ix
Preface xi

PART ONE: SHORT STORIES 1

Chapter 1:   The Scope of the Battlefield 3
Chapter 2:   A Historical Perspective 17
Chapter 3:   Foundations of Faith 32
Chapter 4:   Our Common Enemy 37
Chapter 5:   Why We Believe 48
Chapter 6:   Tough and Courageous Love 53
Chapter 7:   The Raging Battle 58
Chapter 8:   In Unity and Godly Love 65
Chapter 9:   The Prodigal Son 73
Chapter 10: The Spiritual Journey 81
Chapter 11: The Disunity Continues 85
Chapter 12: A Lay Perspective 93
Chapter 13: Wired for God 100
Chapter 14: The Moral Pendulum 106
Chapter 15: The Culture War 114
Chapter 16: Sacred Theism vs. Secular Humanism 119

PART TWO: CHRISTIAN CORE BELIEFS 125

Chapter 17: The Decalogue and Two Commandments 127
Chapter 18: The Three Primary Creeds... 134
Chapter 19: The Lord's Prayer and King David's Prayer............ 142
Chapter 20: The Seven Holy Sacraments or Mysteries............... 152
Chapter 21: The Articles of Religion... 158

In Conclusion... 197
Bibliography... 205

Acknowledgments

The process of writing a book seems always somewhat of a collaborative effort among family and friends. When we are not in collaboration, it is still a personal journey for the author who has often to travel the road alone. When all efforts and sacrifices are completed, a product is produced for better or for worse. In terms of contributions by family and friends, it was the able assistance of my mentor and priest in The Episcopal Church (USA), The Rev. H. Frederick Gough, who has afforded me this priceless favor. It goes without saying that I am indebted to him for assisting me in obtaining my doctor of theology degree. He brings the advice of no fewer equivalents than any university or college professor.

It would be impossible to list all those who over the years have given advice, or mentored, or given their friendship and time to me when lessons were learned. In light of this reality, I wish to acknowledge my wonderful wife Cynthia to whom I have dedicated this book. She has sacrificed much to allow me time to research and write this book. We missed many holidays and special occasions with our children and grandchildren so that I could get my work completed. My parents, Paul and Lorene, were selfless supporters of me and have always encouraged their children to get as much education as possible. I wish to acknowledge my brothers Michael and Ronnie, as well as my daughters Tiffany and Carlyn and my grandchildren Joshua, Grace, Tyler, Savannah, Andrew, and Emily Grace.

Finally, I wish to keep in memory my grandfather-in-law, the late Rev. Dr. A.D Shoemaker, PhD DD, who served as a United

States Army Chaplain (MAJ) in WWII. He was a Southern Methodist minister and will always be fondly remembered. In many ways, my wife and I seem to be following in the footsteps of Dr. and Mrs. Shoemaker. We should be so fortunate.

Preface

This book has been years in the making. I hope it turns out like a good wine that has become more flavorful and rich as it matured over the years. The subject matter is particularly important for our generation, but perhaps more important for our future generations of children and grandchildren. America and the world began significant changes in the twentieth century. Many of those changes were for the better, but sadly many were for the worse. As I think of my parents who were born in the twenties and grew up in a rural environment; I contemplate how fortunate they were to see the first mechanized automobile, the first telephone, the first radio, and the first television, the first interstate highway, and to see the first man walk on the moon. In my own life, I have seen the first eight track stereo, the first citizens band radio, the first cassette, the first compact disc, the first computer, the first drive-through fast food restaurant, the first hand held calculator, the first flat screen television, the internet and so on. Now, stop for a minute and think of your own life span and count the firsts in your life. Seriously, take a moment.

Someone once said that in life we must take the good with the bad. In that case, the bad is the fruits of secular humanism[1] which is a 'philosophy or world view that stresses human values without reference to religion or spirituality.' The concept of original sin is the essence of secular humanism and it traces back to the Garden of Eden. The pace seemed to accelerate during WWI and the cultural

---

[1] Secular Humanism. (1997). Microsoft Encarta 97 Encyclopedia. *Microsoft Encarta 97 Encyclopedia Dictionary Tools.* Redmond, Washington. Microsoft Encarta 97 Encyclopedia.

and societal changes that occurred when our soldiers, sailors and marines came home. No doubt the carefree lifestyle of the Roaring Twenties[2] led to the financial collapse in the late thirties. The Great Depression[3] which lasted from 1929 into WWII had a profound effect on our nation and our way of life. Hard working Americans who lived by a fierce independence and selfsufficient way of life gave way to government programs that were created to make jobs and support people at the taxpayers' expense. Some scholars called these government programs the result of 'creeping socialism' where America and its citizens in contrast had for so long been a self-sufficient capitalist nation. Today, we are a nation that combines both socialism and capitalism. If we consider that secular humanism has had its greatest influence on us in the last century because of the acceleration of the end of the church age, then the seeds were planted after WWI during the Roaring Twenties, and their growth was fertilized after WWII when the arsenal of democracy turned its factories away from military hardware to consumer hardware like washers, dryers and automobiles. Wars have often been the catalyst for change because so much is focused on the results of the political and military outcome. Governmental and economic alliances change our world's outlook because trading partners have new demands and requirements. As a testament to these changes, we bear witness to what the North American Free Trade Agreement (NAFTA) and outsourcing have done to the job market in the United States and the current generation. We have fewer manufacturing positions available to employ those who need jobs to support their families.

Now in Ecclesiastes 1:9 we read, *"that which has been is what will be, that which is done is what will be done, and there is*

---

[2] Roaring Twenties, The. (1997). Microsoft Encarta 97 Encyclopedia. *Microsoft Encarta 97 Encyclopedia Dictionary Tools.* Redmond, Washington. Microsoft Encarta 97 Encyclopedia.

[3] Great Depression, The. (1997). Microsoft Encarta 97 Encyclopedia. *Microsoft Encarta 97 Encyclopedia Dictionary Tools.* Redmond, Washington. Microsoft Encarta 97 Encyclopedia.

nothing new under the sun".[4] This is true because original sin has not changed and with the world population explosion over the last century, we have seen the fruit of secular humanism in great abundance and it is not subsiding. We have increasingly become a self-absorbed society. We are becoming less spiritual which causes us to trust or fear God less. Fear in the biblical sense means to obey and respect God. As we read from Psalms 86:11-13 in the New International Version, *"Teach me your way, O Lord, and I will walk in your truth; give me an undivided heart, that I may fear your name. I will praise you, O Lord my God, with all my heart; I will glorify your name forever, For great is your love toward me; you have delivered me from the debts of the grave."*

As a contrast to secular humanism, I have developed a new idiom called sacred theism. If you interpret secular humanism as a worldly man, then a sacred theism is the Holy Father. My objective is to help people to realize the need for a sacred theistic life and to incorporate that particular lifestyle into their daily lives. Therefore, consider the '*The Pentagon of Faith Sacred Theism vs. Secular Humanism A Christian's Need for the Traditional Faith of Our Fathers* as a set of blueprints. They provide a fortress which will protect us from the forces of secular humanism that are working against the Christian believers in the areas of values and morality.

As you read this book, you will find that it is a part short story, part biography, part journal, part historical document, part theological document, part novel, part essay, part diary and I hope altogether entertaining and informative. I hope this book challenges you to take serious your place in eternity. Some areas are meant to be controversial because I want you to think about your decisions and what impact they will have on your life. It is not intended to be judgmental because judgment is God's purview. It is written to alert you and make you aware of the world around you so you will be a leader not a follower. It is written to encourage you to depart from the secular humanist world of materialism and

---

[4] Believer's Study Bible, The. (1991). The Believer's Study Bible. *The Believer's Study Bible New King James Version.* Thomas Nelson Publishers. Nashville, Tennessee. The Old Testament. King Solomon. Ecclesiastes 9:1. Page 893.

dedicate your life to a sacred theistic world of righteousness. I hope after you have read this book you will have gained strength and courage from its lessons. I hope you also realize that we are in a battle for our souls but we are not alone, we have God with us.

This book is divided into two parts. Part One consists of a number of short stories, or homilies, or articles, or prose that is intended to examine the conflicting values of secular humanism and sacred theism. These individual stories examine the issues from various viewpoints. They will offer commentaries that may or may not offer solutions on how or when the problem can be resolved, if at all, although the solution may be found in another story. These short stories cut across the spectrum and every effort was made to not to leave any stone unturned. They are analytical in their approach. They are designed to help the reader answer any question he or she may have concerning the subject matter. Basically, these stories are designed to aid the reader in such a way as to prepare them to move in the direction of sacred theism. If they begin from the side of a secular humanist or, if they are already living a sacred theistic life, then I hope *The Pentagon of Faith* will strengthen and inspire them to continue to live a sacred way of life.

Many of the issues will be discussed more than once in another short story but here again; this is designed to fully develop the subject. Think of it this way. When you read the four Gospels of the New Testament, do you find that in each one, you are reading the same story over again? Well, yes, there are many instances where each apostle recorded the same story but offered his particular viewpoint. That is precisely what you will experience here in this book. What you will realize over the course of your reading is that you have attained a deeper understanding of the subject at hand. I believe this will better prepare the reader to become more receptive to the core beliefs offered in Part Two of this book. And if you think about the repetition of the stories in the Gospels, then you know that it did not diminish the effect of their lessons, indeed they only enhanced and completed the meaning of what was offered to the reader.

Part Two includes the five major Christian core beliefs. Hence, you will notice the reference to the *Pentagon of Faith* in the title of this book. These core beliefs are in no particular order of theological priority. They are the Ten Commandments, the Three Primary Creeds, the Seven Holy Sacraments, the Lord's Prayer, and the Articles of Religion. There should be no doubt that the pendulum of life has swung in the direction of secular humanism over the last century and accelerated over the last fifty years. It is time for our lives to regain a balance and return to the core Christian values this nation and world needs to stabilize it in the volatile undercurrents that are tearing our society's foundations apart. My ambition is that this book provides a vehicle to help return us to a more sacred theistic way of life. I am promoting and suggesting that the reader find a life of peace and joy that is found in the merits of our human nature as God created us; not in the materialistic emptiness and unhappiness of a life of idolatry which a secular humanist life promotes. This second section identifies the core Christian beliefs in detail and is followed by a notable conclusion and bibliography. After reading this book, my hope and prayer is that your life will take a turn for the better. If you like this book, I hope that you will make it available to your friends so that their lives will equally benefit from the lessons that are taught herein.

PART ONE
Short Stories

Chapter One

The Scope of the Battlefield

> *"My son, forget not my law: but let thine heart keep my commandments: for length of days, and long life, and peace, shall they add to thee".*[5]

Some years ago, not long after the World Trade Center bombing in New York, N.Y. on September 11, 2001, my wife Cynthia and I were shopping in Fayetteville, North Carolina. It is a city that is about an hour's drive north on Interstate 95 from our home in Dillon, South Carolina. I drove to the store entrance of TJ Maxx, one of my wife's favorite department stores, and let her out to go in to begin shopping while I navigated into a parking space. When I exited my vehicle I noticed an attractive family—a husband, a wife and two children, all dressed in traditional Muslim attire. We exchanged pleasantries and it came to pass in our conversation that he was as much a devout Muslim as I was a devout Christian. His wife and children entered the same store where my wife was shopping and he and I remained behind on the sidewalk to discuss theological differences between the Christian and Muslim religions.

---

[5] Holy Bible, The. (2004). The Holy Bible. *The Holy Bible Authorized King James Version.* World Publishing. Nashville, Tennessee. www.worldpublishing.com. The Old Testament. King Solomon. The Book of Proverbs 3:1-2. Page 291.

Understandably, there was a general cloud of suspicion in the air at that time concerning Muslims in America. It was widely reported that a group of Muslims were thought to be responsible for the catastrophe in New York, Washington, DC and rural Pennsylvania. The national press was quickly painting Muslims as our nation's new enemy. My first impression was that he was a brave soul to step out in public wearing traditional Muslim attire. Fayetteville is a military town and home to the United States Army Fort Bragg, United States Pope Air Force Base, the Delta Force Special Operations, and the 82nd Airborne. In fact, it was perhaps his display of courage and bravery that drew me to him.

Several years ago I was awarded a Bachelor of Arts degree in Religion at a noteworthy liberal arts college named Wofford located in Spartanburg, South Carolina. While a student there I considered that I benefited from a better than average education and advanced theological training from professors such as the Department chairman Dr. John Bullard, a Yale Divinity School alumnus, as well as many other highly educated professors. Now as the possessor of this religious background, I thought I could do more than hold my own with respect to the average Christian and even more so compared to a person from another religious discipline. However, this man of the Muslim faith, in defense of his religion, had me on my theological heels, so to speak. I found that I had to dig deep into my intellectual and spiritual resources to respond to his core beliefs and statements with pertinent, thoughtful, and knowledgeable answers. I found that there was some truth to his religious beliefs but they all fell short of the whole truth.

Our exchange of theological mortar fire can be illustrated in the Gospel of St. Matthew's account when Christ was tempted in the wilderness by Satan. Please do not surmise that I am in the least trying to imply here that we were a protagonist versus an antagonist; nor am I implying that he and I were comparable in the same person as Christ or Satan; rather I am citing here to highlight Christ's example to us on how to participate in an exercise such as this, and how one can establish not just the truth but the whole truth, so help us God. The Scripture is written as follows:

> *"Then Jesus was led by the Spirit into the wilderness to be tempted by the devil. And after He had fasted for forty days and forty nights, He then became hungry. And the tempter came and said to Him, 'If you are the Son of God, command that these stones become bread'. But He answered and said, 'It is written, man shall not live on bread alone, but on every word that proceeded out of the mouth of God'. Then the devil took Him into the holy city and had Him stand on the pinnacle of the temple, and said to Him, 'If you are the Son of God, throw yourself down, for it is written, 'He will command His angels concerning You', and 'On their hands they will bear you up, so that you will not strike your foot against a stone'. Jesus said to him, 'On the other hand it is written, "You shall not put the Lord your God to the test'. Again, the devil took Him to a very high mountain and showed Him all the kingdoms of the world and their glory; and he said to Him, 'All these things I will give you, if you fall down and worship me'. Then Jesus said to him, 'Go, Satan! For it is written, 'You shall worship the Lord your God, and serve Him only'. Then the devil left Him; and behold, angels came and began to minister to Him".*[6]

This is certainly a great passage for all Christians to read as it is a great illustration of how a partial truth exhibited by Satan in the preceding passage can miss the point of the whole truth.

---

[6] Today's Parallel Bible. (2000). *Today's Parallel Bible New American Standard Bible Updated.* Zondervan Publishing House. Grand Rapids, Michigan. The New Testament. St. Matthew. The Gospel according to Matthew 4:1-11.Page 2207.

It can be a great exercise on how to find the truth, exhibited and portrayed by Christ. One aspect of this verbal intercourse between Jesus and Satan written in the Gospel of St. Matthew is that Jesus is showing us how we are to confront falsehoods. We do so by quoting Scripture. This should underscore the importance of our daily devotions and Scripture readings as well as our memorization of Holy Scripture.

Herein, abides the paradox where I found myself residing. With humility, I thought that if I were a follower of the Christian faith, and if it were established, based on my background, education and training that I knew more than the average Christian, then how easy it would be for the less knowledgeable Christian to be misled in the truth of the Gospel by false representations. Let's face it, conventional wisdom attests that many Christians attend Church twice a year, typically on Christmas and Easter. They call themselves CEO's, an acronym for Christmas and Easter Only. Still others attend services a few Sundays out of the year. Then there are those who attend regularly. Further still are those who attend every Sunday and who attend an additional service during the week usually on a Wednesday night for a prayer service. I know church attendance is not solely the answer for calling ourselves Christian but are we getting the biblical knowledge we need to confront evil on such limited church attendance? Or do our *laissez-faire,* or casual attitudes cause us to become better known and depicted as 'part time' Christians?

This cannot be a good sign for those meager Christians or for the whole of Christianity in my view. Christians need to have our spirits nourished on a regular basis. Weekly church attendance is designed to supplement our daily worship. Common fellowship with like minded believers exercised through regular church worship and Sunday school provides us a great source for recharging our batteries, so to speak. I know I feel energized and ready for 'battle' for that upcoming week after attending Sunday services. If I miss Sunday service, I feel that something in me seems amiss. For us to take our faith and beliefs so flippantly or consider them so inconsequential and then have the courage to call ourselves Christians, to me, quite frankly, borders on dishonor. Now many of you may rush to judgment considering this statement and call me judgmental. Being judgmental is wrong for a Christian but using good judgment while discerning what is right or wrong is a necessity. So, let's consider these facts. There is an urban legend[7] that claims the Reverend Dr. Billy Graham[8] was asked, "How many people do you think are true Christians?" It is reported that his reply was, "two out of every ten are true Christians". Now, you may think that this is a low number and it represents one out of every five and you have doubts about its accuracy. So, let's examine another example. Dr. D. James Kennedy was quoted as saying, "the vast majority of people who are members of a church in America today are not Christian. I say that without the slightest fear of contradiction. I base it on empirical evidence of twenty-four years of examining thousands of people. I do not know how to calculate vast majority but suffice it to say it is more than less".[9] Now, in reference to Dr. Graham's purported statement, that an urban legend cannot be proven then, let me give you some biblical statistics that can confirm all these statistics. In the *Parable of the Sower,*[10] Christ compares Christians to four categories of soil. These four categories are wayside, rock, thorn, and good soil. Wayside, rock, and thorn Christians will fail to enter into heaven. That is equivalent to three in four. And if we consider the *Parable*

---

[7] Urban Legend. (2002). The American Heritage College Dictionary. *The American Heritage College Dictionary Fourth Edition.* Joseph P. Pickett Vice President and Executive Editor. Published by Houghton Mifflin Company. Boston, Massachusetts. Page 1508.

[8] Graham, Dr. Billy. (2012). *Billy Graham Evangelistic Association.* Evangelist and Minister. Charlotte, North Carolina. www.billygraham.org.

[9] Kennedy, Dr. D. James. (2012). The Way of the Master with Kirk Cameron. May 24, 2006. Coral Ridge Presbyterian Church. Fort Lauderdale, Florida. www.crpc.org. Trinity Broadcasting Network. Santa Ana, California. www.tbn.org.

[10] Disciple's Study Bible. (1988) *Disciple's Study Bible New International Version.* Holman Bible Publishers. A Cornerstone Bible. Nashville, Tennessee. The New Testament. St. Matthew. The Gospel according to Matthew 13:1-23. Pages 1191-1192.

of the Ten Virgins,[11] or *Wise and Foolish Virgins,* then we read that there are only one in two. In this parable, five virgins had their lamps full of oil and five did not. When the bridegroom came and took the five virgins whose oil lamps were full behind the door and closed it, then that was the end. The five virgins whose lamps were empty returned and hammered on the door and said. "Lord, Lord let us in". And His reply was, "I do not know you". The five virgins replied, "but we called you by your name, cast out demons in your name, and did many wonders in your name" and he replied, "again, depart from me, for I do not know you". These are words no Christian wants to hear but regrettably gathering from the statistics previously mentioned, more self-proclaimed Christians will hear these words than those who will not. The question from this passage we should ask ourselves is not if we know Jesus Christ, but does Jesus Christ know us?

Spiritual discipline and adherence to Christian doctrine is as important as the air we breathe. It is the basis of sacred theism. It is important because this is how God made us. We cannot fully function and expect to reach our fullest potential without the presence of God in our everyday lives. Simple and reverent actions with little or no physical demands such as genuflecting are often unknown in many denominational worship services. Of course those with disabilities are not obligated to genuflect[12] nor are the non-Roman or the AngloCatholic body of Christendom. Kneeling or showing the sign of the cross is reflective of the respect and reverence we show to God our Creator. In contrast to this previous statement, Muslims kneel on their prayer rugs five times a day facing Mecca and pray to their God, Allah. They consider it an honor and privilege to worship this way seven days a week not

---

[11] Disciple's Study Bible. (1988) *Disciple's Study Bible New International Version.* Holman Bible Publishers. A Cornerstone Bible. Nashville, Tennessee. The New Testament. St. Matthew. The Gospel according to Matthew 25: 1-13. Page 1215.

[12] Genuflect. (2001). Random House College Dictionary. *Random House Webster's College Dictionary 2nd Revised and Updated Edition.* Random House, Inc. New York, New York. www.randomhouse.com. Page 548.

a burden as many Christians may feel. Many Christians, on the other hand, consider that they are faithful if they attend church services once a week and for one or two hours at best. There is an old saying that says "you get what you pay for". This can be translated, "you get out of it what you put in it" or "no investment, no reward". It appears many Christians believe one or two hours a week is enough investment for God. Yet, in times of trouble, whom do they immediately call? They call on God.

It appears that something is missing in this scenario, don't you think? Something is off course or is not connecting? Why have Christians failed to understand the importance of regular worship and prayer? Where do you think Christians made the wrong turn? Have Christians been led to believe that God is pleased with treating Him as a convenience? Is there any wonder in anyone's mind why this country and this world has drifted along aimlessly and sunk to the spiritual depths that we are now experiencing? In Europe and around the world, Christians are wavering from the relentless secular humanist attacks challenging not only our beliefs but our right to our religious freedoms. It seems impossible to have a polite discussion debating the merits of religion in general or Christianity in specifics. Further it seems that the merits no longer have merit themselves because what seems to matter is that the perceived winner of the debate wins by his or her vocal ability. In other words, if you can shout the loudest, you win or if everyone departs from the debate and you are the last one standing, then you are considered the 'winner'.

In an article entitled, *Christians Under Threat as Radical Islam Spreads in New Middle East*, author Henry Reske writes, "attacked by mobs and terrorists, repressed by the growing popularity of fundamentalist Islamic law and cut off from crucial business ties, Christians are fleeing the Middle East in an unprecedented exodus".[13] It now seems that tolerance is the byword for today's politically correct establishment but it is evident that tolerance

---

[13] Newsmax. (October 24 2011). *Christians Under Threat as Radical Islam Spreads in New Middle East*. Henry J. Reske. America's News Page. 2012 Newsmax Media, Inc. All rights reserved. www.Newsmax.com.

is acceptable for every religion including non-religions such as atheists except for Christianity. Atheists have more rights now than Christians and the irony is that atheism is defined as "not believing in any God". What has happened to our United States Constitutional First Amendment that allows us, among other things, the Freedom of Religion and Speech?[14] If one mentions Christianity in public anymore, can he or she be considered tolerant? I think not yet we somehow call this tolerant. It seems we can mention any other religion or non-religion in public except Christianity. One would think based on the printed media and public discourse that there is an underlying prejudice against Christianity and those who practice its precepts. One would also be led to believe that there is a bias against the Christian and Jewish people. I include the Jewish people because Jesus was a Jew and Christianity has its foundations in Judaism. Someone needs to look up the definition of tolerance where this is in practice. Many of you may find these statements incredible so let me cite some statistics written in a recent USA Today article entitled, *Losing My Religion isn't Just a Song: It's Life*[15]. The statistics in this article are alarming for any Christian. The author, Cathy Lynn Grossman, states that the attitude most Americans have toward religion is "so what"? She quotes Mark Silk, a professor of religion at Trinity College in Hartford, Connecticut as saying, "the real dirty secret of religiosity in America is that there are so many people for whom spiritual interest thinking about ultimate questions is minimal". LifeWay Research[16] in Nashville, Tennessee reports that forty-six percent of Americans never wonder whether they will go to heaven. It sounds like the making of a good country music song except for the fact that this is eternally serious business. Why do so

---

[14] U. S. Constitution, The. (1776). *The United States Constitution First Amendment.* Legal Information Institute Open Access to Law Since 1992. Cornell University Law School. www.law.cornell.edu.

[15] USA Today Newspaper. (2012). Column: 'Losing My Religion isn't Just a Song: It's Life', Cathy Lynn Grossman, January 13, 2012, Life Section, page 2.

[16] LifeWay Research. (2001-2012). LifeWay Christian Resources of the Southern Baptist Convention. Nashville, Tennessee. www.lifeway.com.

many believe we are only in a temporary existence on this earth? The fact of creation is that we will all live for eternity. The question we should ask ourselves is where we will spend that eternity. The Bible as well as other religious documents from other religions is clear. It will be in heaven or in hell. But the choice is ours based on how we live our lives. If we live for ourselves in a secular humanist way then we will go to hell. If we live our lives for God as a sacred theism way and ask His Son to be our savior and repent of our sins, then we will go to live in Heaven for eternity and live as sons of the King. Additionally, a Baylor University[17] Religion Survey concluded that forty-four percent of Americans spend no time seeking "eternal wisdom" and another nineteen percent said "it is useless to search for meaning". These statistics portray a sad commentary on America for it was these Christian core beliefs that made our country strong. These statistics are alarming trends in America and if we wish to call ourselves a Christian nation, then there is strong evidence that we are becoming anything but a nation of the Judeo-Christian values which were the core beliefs of our founding fathers. This is another reason why every Christian needs to return to the traditional faith of our fathers.

As you can see from these statistics, this report gives us the results of the effective secularism of the people in America. They are the result of years of our feeding on secular humanism and our straying away from sacred theism. If the Middle East is known as the Cradle of Civilization; and although Armenia claims to be the first Christian nation, then Europe is at least the incubator of Christianity which grew to dominance after the fall of the Roman Empire in 476 A.D. However, the public onslaught and intolerance against Christianity has effectively made the Christian religion a minority in Europe today and it is quickly developing the same way in the United States. This effective and orchestrated campaign called the 'Culture War' is led by academia, the media, public legislators and even unsuspecting businesses that acquiesce to their threats of protest and have an agenda to wipe out the values

---

[17] Baylor University. (1845). A private Southern Baptist University. Waco, Texas. www.baylor.edu.

of Christian beliefs. Two world wars in the last century on the continent of Europe have had a negative effect on the Europeans. This dwindling of Judeo-Christian values is coming to America and before it overtakes us, we Christians need to return to the faith of our fathers if we are to survive with the freedom to practice our religious freedom and way of life. This is a clarion call to rise up and be counted.

The other day my wife and I were driving to Florence to purchase some Bibles in bulk to have available for my church. She has always been a good listener and "sounding board" for the ideas that God reveals to me. I had been thinking for some time about the puzzle about the chicken and the egg. Which came first? Then I was thinking about another puzzle. Does life imitate art, or does art imitate life? I will leave the answers to the reader but these two questions help us to tackle the problem we now face. In contemplating the *Scope of the Battlefield*, have we allowed man to set the agenda or have we let God set the agenda in terms of our worship? If we are setting our own agenda then it appears we have become our own worst enemy. Certainly regular selfanalysis is productive to determine where we stand in life as well as where we stand with God. Adam and his descendants were created with a purpose to worship and glorify God. Whatever vocation we choose is irrelevant, since our single most important purpose in life is giving God our continued worship, adoration and praise. Think about it this way. In your daily prayer life, do you find that you spend your time in prayer *mostly* asking Him for something? Or do you spend your time in prayer mostly praising and worshiping Him? If you are honest with yourself then I think you will begin to see the paradox wherein we find ourselves. Are we the chicken or egg or are we life or art? Our worship has developed where we want to be on the receiving end and not the giving end. God wants us to give Him our talents and gifts, not the other way around where God is always giving. Perhaps then we will begin to have worship services that honor our Heavenly Father only and not ourselves. Actually that type of service has been around for several hundred years. It is a liturgical service that incorporates both the word and the sacrament. So as we examine the battlefield, we need first to cleanse ourselves before we march against the enemy. If we focus on Sacred Theism[18] rather than Secular Humanism,[19] then we have begun that journey. Sacred theism is an idiom that I have created to counterbalance secular humanism and it is defined as the worship of our Creator and only Religion Survey concluded God, our Holy Father. When we turn our attentions to God and not ourselves, then we become connected to Him and our world that He created for us. By contrast, secular humanism has been around and talked about for ages since its roots are found in original sin. It is the condition where man basically becomes part of the world. God expects us to live in this world, but not to become a part of it. This distinction is difficult for many to understand and comprehend. Another way to look at it is a secular humanist or worldly man living on this earth for his own purpose in a closed universe where he is master versus a sacred theist or Godly man who abides by the precepts of sacred theism seeking God in an open universe where God is master. One person sees everything through the lens of the secular (man), while the other person sees everything through the lens of the sacred (God).

These opposing views of man's purpose in this world took a turn as we will see in the following article. According to the Encyclopedia Britannica, "the movement toward secularism has been in progress during the entire course of modern history and has often been viewed as being anti-Christian and anti-religious. In the latter half of the 20th century, some theologians began advocating secular Christianity. They suggested that Christianity should not be concerned only with sacred and the other worldly, but that people should find in the world the opportunity to promote

---

[18] Sacred Theism. (2012). The Pentagon of Faith. The Pentagon of Our Faith: Secular Humanism vs. Sacred Theism A Christian's need for the Traditional Faith of Our Fathers. Lulu.com Original Idiom. Rev. Donald R. Hayes. Page 18.

[19] Humanism. (2001). Random House College Dictionary. *Random House Webster's College Dictionary 2nd Revised and Updated Edition*. Random House, Inc. New York, New York. www.randomhouse.com. Page 642.

Christian values".[20] The last sentence is an attempt to mask the fact that secular humanism promotes man as supreme and ultimately a self-serving individual who is opposed to Christian principles and values and certainly contrary to what God teaches us in the Holy Scriptures. What makes this last part difficult to comprehend is that the author attributes this view to some members of the clergy. This is sad but true that many clergy in that time period did turn to the secular world and walked away from the sacred world they were commissioned to teach and defend.

The Rev. Jim Bakker of the PTL Club[21] program comes to mind as an example of yielding to worldly pursuits and we witnessed to his extravagantly materialistic lifestyle and saw with amazement when it came crashing down. And then the floodgates opened, for there were many more preachers who became victims to their own selfish behaviors or false theology. And the Rev. Jim Bakker was preceded by Bishop John Shelby Spong,[22] the retired Episcopal Bishop of Newark, New Jersey who taught that the virgin birth of Jesus Christ was scientifically impossible and therefore a falsehood. He continued to challenge traditional Christian teachings by supporting the ordination of homosexuals to the priesthood. These leaders in the name of Christ have made many followers of their brands and the result is a major stain on the reputation of Christianity and ultimately how it reflects on our Savior Jesus Christ and our Heavenly Father. However, the majority of clergy are virtuous and noble rather than the exceptions such as the Rev.

---

[20] Secularism. (2001). Random House College Dictionary. Random House Webster's College Dictionary 2nd Revised and Updated Edition. Random House, Inc. New York, New York. www.randomhouse.com. Page 1189.
[21] Messner, Tammy Faye. (2009). Encyclopedia Britannica. *Encyclopedia Britannica 2009 Deluxe Edition.* Chicago: Encyclopedia Britannica.
[22] Spong, Bishop John Shelby. (1995). Apologia. *What's wrong with Bishop Spong? Laymen Rethink the Scholarship of John Shelby Spong.* Wellington Christian Apologetics Society. Michael Bott and Jonathan Sarfati. www.creation.com.

Jimmy Swaggart,[23] an Assemblies of God minister, who like Bakker built a media empire that disintegrated after allegations of sexual misbehavior and financial wrongdoing led to his downfall. These soap opera stories which always seem to gather the television and newspaper headlines put an unsavory view on religion, especially Christianity. It was not just these Pentecostal[24] ministers, who emphasize the working of the Holy Spirit and interpret the Bible literally, like Bakker and Swaggart who led many astray and left them disillusioned; but in the last decade we have been inundated with the sin of pedophilia,[25] or the crime of sex with a child by an adult, which was revealed, but not limited to, the priesthood of the Roman Catholic Church. In total these wayward representatives of Christianity have brought Christianity into doubt and now we see that they have turned millions of people away from Christianity while supporting alternatives to the lessons of sacred theism. There were some successes during the 1960s and 70s, when the Rev. Dr. Jerry Falwell[26], a fundamentalist Southern Baptist minister from Lynchburg, Virginia and founder of the Moral Majority[27] and Thomas Road Baptist Church, led hundreds of thousands of the faithful in the traditional values found in Christianity and sacred theism. Dr. Falwell was 'opposed to abortion, feminism, gay rights, and other causes associated with cultural and social

---

[23] Jimmy Swaggart. (1988). The Fall of Jimmy Swaggart. People Magazine. A division of Time Warner Publications. Archives. Article by Joanne Kaufman March 07, 1988 Vol. 29, No. 9. www.people.com.

[24] Pentecostal. (2010). Christianity The First Three Thousand Years. Viking. Published by the Penguin Group. Penguin Group (USA), Inc. New York, New York. Diarmaid MacCulloch. Page 965.

[25] Pedophilia. (2002). The American Heritage College Dictionary. The American Heritage College Dictionary Fourth Edition. Joseph P. Pickett, Vice President and Executive Editor. Houghton Mifflin Company. Boston, Massachusetts. Page 1026.

[26] Falwell, Jerry. (1995). Church History in Plain Language. *Updated 2 Edition Church History in Plain Language.* Thomas Nelson Publishers. Nashville, Tennessee. Bruce L. Shelley. Page 477.

[27] Falwell, Jerry. (1995). Church History in Plain Language. *Updated 2 Edition Church History in Plain Language.* Thomas Nelson Publishers. Nashville, Tennessee. Bruce L. Shelley. Page 477.

transformation'[28], exhibited in secular humanism. Yet he was constantly under attack and had to defend himself from a secular humanist media and self-centered and materialistic society.

Look how man changed when he went from his sacred theism views to his secular humanism views. It was often reported that the 1980's was the materialistic decade. And it did not stop there. It continues to this day. Music largely reflects the views of our society and if you remember that one of the top musical pop hits in 1985 was *Material Girl* by Madonna.[29] This song underscores the results of a secular humanist society which clearly makes this argument certain. I do not suggest that music is the only vehicle that promotes secular humanism in our society. Certainly, Hollywood and Broadway have a mighty effect on what we believe and how it affects our morals and how we behave. Television was once considered to be designed for family entertainment. I am concerned by anyone's honest opinion, television has lost its family appeal because there seems to be no check or balance in terms of what is aired. And television programs are not limited to the degradation in moral behavior. Commercials add to the long list of sexual promiscuity, sexual innuendo, and curse words. We have an uphill battle if we are to return to a standard of a decent and moral way of life. To adopt a life of sacred theism is not for the fainthearted and I would not tell you it will be easy to live that way for all the pressures from so many institutions are converging against Christianity. However, you must make a stand for the righteous way of life and prevail for our children and grandchildren's sake if not for ours only. And, I dare say, choose life and sacred theism or chose death and remain in secular humanism.

---

[28] Falwell, Jerry. (1995). Church History in Plain Language. *Updated 2 Edition Church History in Plain Language.* Nashville, Tennessee. Bruce L. Shelley. Page 478.

[29] Madonna. (2009). Encyclopedia Britannica. Encyclopedia Britannica 2009 Deluxe Edition. Chicago: Encyclopedia Britannica.

Chapter Two

A Historical Perspective

"Let not mercy and truth forsake thee; bind them about thy neck: write them upon the table of thine heart: So shalt thou find favour and good understanding in the sight of God and man".[30]

Where did the disconnect start and where are we today? Many think it began with and during the Protestant Reformation[31] in 1517 AD and ended in 1648 AD with the Treaty or Peace of Westphalia[32] that ended the Thirty Years War.[33] Some would say it dates back to the early Church where doctrinal issues were being put to the test and heresies were regularly addressed by the apostles and their followers. Unfortunately, while many think these apostasies were disposed of, to the contrary, several of these heresies never totally dissolved and often they are repackaged and renamed in forms like secular humanism that we witness today.

---

[30] Holy Bible, The. (2004). The Holy Bible. *The Holy Bible Authorized King James Version.* World Publishing. Nashville, Tennessee. www.worldpublishing.com. The Old Testament, King Solomon, The Book of Proverbs 3:3-4, page 291.

[31] Protestant Reformation, The. (1995). Church History in Plain Language. *Updated 2nd Edition Church History In Plain Language.* Thomas Nelson Publishers. Nashville, Tennessee. Bruce L. Shelley. Pages 237-246.

[32] Westphalia, Peace of. (2010). *Christianity The First Three Thousand Years.* Viking. Published by the Penguin Group. Penguin Group (USA), Inc. New York, New York. Diarmaid MacCulloch. Page 647.

[33] Thirty Years' War. (2009). Encyclopedia Britannica. *Encyclopedia Britannica 2009 Deluxe Edition.* Chicago: Encyclopedia Britannica.

Since the issue of secular humanism versus sacred theism is the paradox we face from the historical and religious viewpoint, I have decided to commence this book's discussion beginning with the Protestant Reformation.

The fires of the Reformation were fueled by clerical abuses in office and vocation that violated moral and ethical laws. Some of the "crimes" were things such as selling indulgences or marrying outside of the Sacrament of Holy Matrimony and the church; or having families and fathering children outside of wedlock, or giving family members patronage jobs in the church; or other abuses from the lowest to the highest levels of the clerical ladder. Then the spark that ignited the reformers occurred when a priest nailed to the doors of the Castle Church in Wittenberg, Germany his *Ninety-five Theses on the Power and Efficacy of Indulgences*[34] on October 31, 1517. Roman Catholic Father Martin Luther opposed many of the abuses he witnessed in the church. He also found that he also opposed many of the doctrines and traditions of the Catholic Church including ceremonies, rituals and customs as well as ecclesiastical structures that included the lesser Holy Sacraments.

Anglican reformers included Archbishop Thomas Cranmer who penned the Book of Common Prayer[35] in 1549 which is only slightly modified from its original form and is still in service today in the Anglican Communion. Personally, I consider the Anglican Book of Common Prayer to be the second most important book which has ever been written aside from the Holy Bible. It has had a positive effect on countless millions of the Christian faithful over the last five centuries. Many other reformers followed Cranmer including John Wesley[36] who is credited with founding

---

[34] Ninety-five Theses. (2010). *Christianity The First Three Thousand Years.* Viking. Published by the Penguin Group. Penguin Group (USA), Inc. New York, New York. Diarmaid MacCulloch. Page 604.

[35] The Book of Common Prayer. (1549). the first Archbishop of the Church of England, Thomas Cranmer. Publisher and composer, writer and editor.

[36] Wesley, John. (2010). *Christianity The First Three thousand Years.* Viking. Published by the Penguin Group. Penguin Group (USA), Inc. New York, New York. Diarmaid MacCulloch. Page 806.

the Methodist[37] movement but remained a priest of the Anglican Church until his death. His brother Charles Wesley[38], also a priest, wrote many of the most beloved hymns that are in continuous use today by many Protestant denominations.

Prior to the Protestant Reformation, it was not uncommon for an average Christian to worship several times a day and even more so for cloistered monks. If we reference the Anglican Breviary, we find it contains the Divine Office of the Western Church as we bear witness to the early Christians who were called to worship from six to eight times a day depending on the season. According to the worship schedule, these times became known as Prime, Terce, Sext, Nones, Matins, Lauds, Vespers, Nocturn and Compline.[39] When the first Anglican Book of Common Prayer was written and produced by Archbishop Thomas Cranmer in 1549 AD, he was an active participant in the Reformation. However, he pared the number of daily offices from nine to two services by combining the offices and giving them the titles of Morning Prayer[40] and Evening Prayer.[41]

In preparation for attaining my Master of Sacred Theology, I spent three days training at Mepkin Abby in Moncks Corner, South Carolina living among Trappist Monks[42]. They are a Roman

---

[37] Methodist. (2010). *Christianity The First Three Thousand Years.* Published by the Penguin Group. Penguin Group (USA), Inc. New York, New York. Diarmaid MacCulloch. Page 140.

[38] Wesley, Charles. (2010). *Christianity The First Three Thousand Years.* Viking. Published by the Penguin Group. Penguin Group (USA), Inc. Diarmaid MacCulloch. New York, New York. Page 104.

[39] Breviary, The Anglican. (1998). Frank Gavin Liturgical Foundation, Inc. *The Anglican Breviary.* The Lakeside Press.

[40] Prayer, The Book of. (1952). John Wallace Suter, Custodian. *The Order for Daily Morning Prayer.* The Seabury Press. Greenwich, Connecticut. Page 3.

[41] Prayer, The Book of. (1952) John Wallace Suter, Custodian. *The Order of Daily Evening Prayer.* The Seabury Press. Greenwich, Connecticut. Page 21.

[42] Trappist Monks. (2010). *Christianity The First Three Thousand Years.* Viking. Published by the Penguin Group. Penguin Group (USA). New York, New York. Diarmaid MacCulloch. Page 88.

Catholic Religious Order of the Reformed Cistercians[43] of the Strict Observance. One anonymous Trappist Monk was credited as saying, *"there are two main pitfalls on the road to mastery of the art of prayer. If a person gets what he asks for, his humility is in danger, if he fails to get what he asks for, he is apt to lose confidence. Indeed, no matter whether prayer seems to be succeeding or failing, humility and confidence are two virtues which are absolutely essential"*[44]. The Trappist monks from Mepkin Abby and all cloistered monks continue the practice and observance of this pre-Reformation ritual of the daily offices. Their daily routine begins at 3:00am and ends at 8:00pm. I consider it a high water mark for me in my spiritual journey as I participated with these monks in this daily ritual. After three days, I realized that I was more attuned to God than at any other time in my life. The primary lesson I learned is that when we are talking or listening to the radio or television we cannot possibly hear God when he speaks to us. Only when we are in a moment of silence can we hear God speak to us. This is an important lesson for us to learn and if we apply it to our daily lives and if we couple it with prayer and meditation, we can become better disciples of God's purpose for us. Then we begin to develop a lifestyle adhering to the principles of sacred theism.

To this Anglican priest, the Protestant Reformation addressed some important issues and abuses facing the Roman Catholic Church. Certainly, these abuses needed to be corrected and they were long overdue. In hindsight, the long-term result of the Reformation on the Roman Catholic Church as well as the Protestant Churches it spawned in general is mixed. The corrections were so extreme in some cases that they overcompensated for many of the church's transgressions. In addition, the Reformation opened the door to a slippery slope of what has evolved today into a diluted Christian

---

[43] Cistercians Order. (2010). *Christianity The First Three Thousand Years.* Viking. Published by the Penguin Group. Penguin Group (USA), Inc. New York, New York. Diarmaid MacCulloch. Page 389.

[44] Encyclopedia of Religious Quotations. (1966). *The Encyclopedia of Religious Quotations Edited and Compiled by Frank S. Mead.* Fleming H. Revell Company. Westwood, New Jersey. Page 348.

practice of worship. For this reason, I view the Reformation more as a "revolution" because it was more than reform; it was a total revolt against all things catholic.

Now the Anglican Church did not go as far as some reformers had wanted, indeed they took the best from both sides of the Protestant Reformers and the Roman Catholics and found a middle way they call the "via media".[45] As an example, the Anglicans kept many of the traditions, rites and ceremonies but made the necessary corrections in the areas of clerical abuse. One of the biggest changes was that they allowed the clergy to marry. As for the reformers, for instance, the lectionary was largely dismissed so that Scripture reading for any reformed protestant church is largely chosen at total random except the Methodist, Lutheran, and Anglican Churches. I know that systems have been incorporated but by and large the system is diluted from the liturgical denominations. There is no traditional uniformity or consistency in the Scriptures or in many protestant churches that conduct services without a liturgy. They have largely created their own traditions of worship.

Reformer Martin Luther determined that five of the seven sacraments were not ordained by Christ in the Gospel and thus were relatively dismissed or practiced sparingly at all. Only Holy Communion and Holy Baptism survived Martin Luther's changes largely because they are the only ones explicitly ordained by Jesus and written about in the Scriptures. Luther did keep Penance as a sacrament but lessened the value of the remaining four sacraments.

The Protestant Reformation encouraged a greater focus on the written Word. The advent of the printing press allowed many people the opportunity to read the Bible for themselves in their own language rather than hearing it from a member of clergy. These combined efforts ushered in a threshold where men began to develop their own ways of worship apart from traditional services. This prepared a way for anyone to interpret the Holy Scriptures. For this reason about a dozen main line denominations

---

[45] Via Media. (1997). Microsoft Encarta 97 Encyclopedia. *Microsoft Encarta 97 Encyclopedia Dictionary Tools.* Redmond, Washington. Microsoft Encarta 97 Encyclopedia.

developed. And the metamorphosis did not end with the Protestant Reformation.

The metamorphosis or splintering has continued and today there are thousands of independent Christian churches with no allegiance to any particular order or denomination. In a way these independent churches are viewed as orphans of the Church. This would be a great disappointment to the founders of the Reformation. But it comes as a result of the Protestant Reformation. As my maternal grandfather, Aaron Moody, a Southern Baptist deacon and nephew of a Southern Methodist minister named Tapley Moody, would say, "every Tom, Dick, and Harry" thinks he can start a church. These independent churches espouse their unique interpretation of the Holy Scriptures and often they are led by untrained lay ministers whose intentions are good, noble, and sincere but they lack the theological training that would help them to realize when they have fallen into apostasy. It is understandably easy to misinterpret Scripture. These independent church followers are far removed from the liturgical traditions of the church and they often look at them with a high degree of skepticism which I might add, is unfortunate. From the Roman Catholic perspective, they are lost sheep.

There is another trend that is in the fast lane. Marketing gurus use the internet for a fast buck and many aspiring preachers purchase their degrees from what is called a 'diploma mill'. It seems for a few hundred dollars, and a short test or a short term paper; one is allowed to claim they have earned a legitimate theological degree. This is a recipe for disaster since now the newly minted preacher with his 'diploma' in hand can go out and open a new church. It seems what complicates this situation is how the IRS views a church. Anyone can call themselves a church according to the government. This adds to an already complicated problem and opens the door for more apostasy because there is no structure. For all the criticism of the traditional church, at least there are checks and balances for the preparing of people for the vocation of clergy. Preachers are treated no different than any other profession. Some students make the grade and some do not. This is a seasoned method that is tried and true. The best prepared students survive the gantlet.

The Christian church today is in a crisis. I recently attended a clergy conference in Pinehurst, NC where I learned that there are fifteen hundred ordained clergy from all Protestant denominations who are leaving the clerical vocation per month in the United States. This equates to eighteen thousand former members of clergy leaving the church each year. Our traditional seminaries cannot possibly keep up with this pace of departure in order to replace trained and qualified clergy. Either there will be no one to serve the churches responsibly or the clergy will not be well-trained which is a formula for disaster and apostasy. If we add the diluted doctrine running amok in the traditional seminaries over the last fifty years, then we see that the Christian church is teetering on a deep abyss. The current situation is broken on every level and is in dire need of repair.

Ironically, in contrast there seems to be a nontraditional church opening weekly. New churches have been on the increase so that today it seems we find a "new" protestant church on every corner like convenience stores or gasoline stations. The question that everyone should ask is what kind of theology is being preached or taught in our seminaries. It appears that their instruction has missed the mark in adequately or properly preparing new clergymen for their vocation. The void of male recruits for the ministry is quickly being filled by female ministers. However, this trend is not limited to the ordained clergy since it is happening in other vocations such as law and medicine and has been the trend for the last few decades.

Many Protestant Churches find it necessary to regularly reinvent themselves. For instance, five of the seven Holy Sacraments were largely devalued because of the reforms of the Protestant Reformation. Consequently, many mainstream protestant churches do not observe these sacraments on a regular basis. Their reason is somewhat valid as only Holy Communion and Holy Baptism were ordained by Christ in the New Testament. What they miss though is that the other five sacraments of Holy Matrimony, Holy Orders,

Confirmation, Unction and Penance are strongly alluded to and are therefore valid. In fact, a sacrament is defined as 'an outward and visible sign of an inward and spiritual grace'. All five 'minor' sacraments meet these criteria.

Now that sacraments have been treated as major and minor and thus diluted, the worship practices that are the hallmark in liturgical churches for hundreds of years have faded in the non-liturgical churches. Many do not even practice the observance of one of the major sacraments, Holy Communion or Holy Eucharist on a weekly or monthly basis. Quarterly communion services have become the norm for many and now those are being challenged as too often. If I am not mistaken, my understanding of communion is that Jesus said, *"and when he had given thanks, he brake it, and said, Take eat: this is my body, which is broken for you: this do I remembrance of me. After the same manner also he took the cup, when he had supped, saying, this cup is the new testament on my blood: this do ye, as oft as ye drink it in remembrance of me"*.[46] In this case I believe we should observe the Holy Eucharist as often as possible, not as seldom as possible. This is a good example of the diluted state to which many Christian churches have evolved with respect to doctrine and practice. The church councils, vestries, deacons, elder boards and committees have let the Culture War[47] infiltrate our religious bodies and we have headed down the road of secular humanism. We need do an about face and return to the practice and observance of sacred theism where we are lead by the traditional faith of our fathers. A section in Part Two is devoted to the seven sacraments.

Other changes that stemmed from the Protestant Reformation were that traditional and ancient liturgies which incorporate

---

[46] Holy Bible, The. (1996). The Holy Bible. *The Holy Bible New King James Version. The New Testament.* Broadman & Holman Publishers. Nashville, Tennessee. St. Paul. The first Letter of Paul to the Corinthians 11:24-25. Page 1010.

[47] Culture War, The. (1997). Microsoft Encarta 97 Encyclopedia. *Microsoft Encarta 97 Encyclopedia Dictionary Tools.* Redmond, Washington. Microsoft Encarta 97 Encyclopedia.

custom and ritual were essentially thrown out or omitted. And the reforms did not end here. They have slowly chiseled away at our traditional practices and customs until this day and they have not abated. It seems that each successive generation deems it to be their right and privilege to make their mark on the traditional worship service by modifying or changing the way it is practiced. Subsequently there have developed great chasms in protestant nonliturgical services which have become filled with various forms of music and increasingly greater degrees of drama such as plays, acts, testimonies, or rock band concerts. It seems that entertainment has become the norm and not the exception. It goes without saying, when you delete half of the traditional service including the observance of the Holy Eucharist, you have to fill the void with something and usually the easiest way to fill the void is to include music. Lately, this has spread into many traditional liturgical denominations as well where they are offering blended services or nontraditional services.

The members of the non-liturgical Protestant denominations seem to have lost their compass and are floating aimlessly in a sea of discontent or malcontent. Many are struggling with their Gospel mission and are looking for unorthodox ways to fill their church pews. Some have now resorted to offering coffee and doughnuts before and during their services and changing their dress code to casual. Tongue in cheek, "do you think popcorn and sodas or nachos and cheese are far behind"?

Consequently, worship services have now become arenas for entertainment, not worship. Therefore, since many have apparently lost their way, their members are leaving their church to search for a worship service that has meaning and truth. This presents a treacherous passage for those Christians who are not grounded in the fundamental values and beliefs of Christianity. Remember, in the last section, *The Scope of the Battlefield*, I wrote about a situation where I was confronted by a Muslim whose teachings were very compelling. If I had not known the whole truth of the Scriptures from all my days growing up in the church and from my undergraduate training, I could have easily been persuaded to adopt his religious beliefs because they were compelling and very logical. I must admit that my comparative religion course as well as my apologetics course helped me considerably, but my greatest preparation was that I had a fair knowledge of the Holy Scriptures. I distinctly remember the moment, when I found myself back on my heels, that the Holy Spirit reminded me of a verse and helped me to address and counter the partial truths that I was hearing. The verse I remembered is from I John 4:4 and is written, "Ye are of God, little children, and have overcome them: because greater is He that is in you than he who is in the world".[48] Again, if we remember the Scripture where Christ was tempted by Satan, who quoted only parts of the Scripture, that Christ was able to discern Satan's falsehoods because he knew the whole truth found in the Scripture.

This is the peril that is faced by the untrained or unknowledgeable members of the church. These are the members of the Christian church who do not attend regularly and remain unschooled in the Christian truths. They are the ones who remain on mother's milk and never mature beyond infancy in their religious knowledge and wisdom. If only they read a daily devotion and practiced a life of sacred theism. It becomes more difficult especially when they strike out on their own. Unfortunately, there are several breakaway churches that are headed wholeheartedly in the wrong direction and some are now combining Christianity with different religions into a single service. And our mainstream denominational seminaries appear to be supporting this lost venture. I read a news article on the internet not long ago that reported St. Luke's Seminary at The University of the South[49] in Sewanee, Tennessee has taken the Christian Cross out of the chapel altogether except for special occasions. It seems that the

---

[48] Holy Bible, The. (1991). The Holy Bible. *The Holy Bible King James Version.* Holman Bible Publishers. Nashville, Tennessee. The New Testament. St. John. I John 4:4. Page 1257.

[49] Sewanee: The University of the South. (1878). Sewanee: The University of the South The School of Theology. Seminary of the Protestant Episcopal Church. Sewanee, Tennessee. www.sewanee.edu.

cross is there for "window dressing" and has no symbolic purpose. Recently, it was reported that Vanderbilt University[50] is now allowing atheists into all their student organizations including religious. What an irony, that an atheist becomes a member of a religious club when the definition of atheist is one who does not recognize a god or religion. Atheists do not believe in a God, so why be in a club that worships a God? I personally have seen books on the Buddhism and Muslim religions on the shelves of the bookstore at the National Cathedral[51] in Washington, DC. This coincides with a new movement to create one faith and one world religion by combining the best of all religions. This is a blatant assault on Christianity and is no less hypocrisy and apostasy. People are being led astray in record numbers. We have no one to blame but ourselves. We can correct the course, but it may take a superhuman effort and we may not succeed in the short term. Essentially, the seeds of apostasy were planted in the Garden of Eden and few generations ago they made dramatic advances so it may take a few more generations to correct, if they can be corrected at all. We do have in our power the ability to control our own destiny and this would be a great triumph if we could turn things around but it takes many stones to build the church. And if we get our hearts and minds right with God and He leads us, there is no question that we can succeed in returning to the traditional faith of our fathers.

Everywhere but in a few churches today we see that Christians are yearning for traditional values. Fortunately, the traditional liturgical services and sacraments are offered weekly at Anglican Protestant, Roman Catholic, Eastern Orthodox and Evangelical Lutheran Churches because a doctrine of the real Presence of Jesus Christ is in the Eucharist. To a lesser liturgical degree are the Southern Baptists, the United Methodists and the Presbyterian

---

[50] Vanderbilt University. (1875). The Divinity School, Vanderbilt University. Nashville, Tennessee. www.vanderbilt.edu.

[51] Washington National Cathedral, The. (1907). Open to all religions but administered by The Protestant Episcopal Church in America. Washington, District of Columbia. www.washingtonnationalcathedral.org.

Churches in America who offer the Eucharist more regularly than other Protestant denominations but view it more as a memorial. Recently reported on the website of the Anglican Church in North America (ACNA)[52] was a story that was broadcast on the Christian Broadcast Network (CBN)[53] in a segment that aired on Friday December 16, 2011, reporting that young people across America were flocking to Anglican churches. Heather Sells, the CBN reporter, wrote that for *"decades young people have flocked to seeker-friendly churches that feature culturally relevant services and a casual environment. Now, a new denomination (ACNA) that emphasizes tradition and centuries of old sacraments and practices is drawing them in"*.[54] This is evidence that people are searching for the truth of the gospel and it has been delivered continuously by those who continue to practice the ancient and traditional, tried and truly tested observances that our orthodox founding fathers had observed. These are the services that our great, great, great grandfathers have passed on to us. This type of worship does not grow old and it is still relevant today as it was several hundred years ago. Traditional services that observe ancient rituals and customs have their roots in early Christianity and were developed by our ancient Church Fathers[55] such as St. Augustine of Hippo, St. John Chrysostom, Origen of Alexandria, St. Clement of Rome, St. Ignatius of Antioch, St. Polycarp of Smyrna, St. Athanasius of Alexandria, Tertullian, St. Irenaeus of Lyons, St. Ambrose of Milan, and St, Jerome to name a few.

The very nature and genesis of non-liturgical Protestant services are that they are designed to focus on the Word from

---

[52] ACNA. (2008). *The Anglican Church in North America*. Anglicanchurch.net. Archbishop Robert Duncan. Ambridge, Pennsylvania.

[53] CBN. (1960). The Christian Broadcast Network. *The 700 Club*. Pat Robertson, Founder. Virginia Beach, Virginia.

[54] CBN. (1960). The Christian Broadcast Network. *The 700 Club*. Heather Sells, videographer. Documentary aired on December 16, 2011. Virginia Beach, Virginia. Cbn.com.

[55] Eusebius' Ecclesiastical History. (2011). *Eusebius' Ecclesiastical History Complete and Unabridged New Updated Edition*. Hendrickson Publishers. Translated by C.F. Cruse. Peabody, Massachusetts.

Scripture while the liturgical services focus not solely on the Word, but equally on the Word *and* Sacrament. This is why, in liturgical services, one will witness a combination of the ante-communion (hearing of the Word) and the communion (receiving and sharing in the sacrament). Liturgical services have a penitential nature to their form of worship. In other words, unlike the non-liturgical protestant services who gather to receive validation of their existence and lessons on Christian behavior, liturgical worship gathers members together on their knees (genuflecting) to seek redemption and offer worship and praise to our Heavenly Father. Another way to look at it is comparing the two forms of services. In a liturgical service, members are laying bare themselves, their gifts and their talents and worshipping Christ the Son and God the Heavenly Father who brings them into His grace. In non-liturgical services, the lessons are being taught from the pulpit to the congregation; not from the congregation to Christ at the altar seeking repentance and reconciliation by the church member from the Holy Father.

Perhaps Martin Luther, the Roman Catholic priest who is considered the father of the Protestant Reformation, tended to focus on the word rather that the sacrament. It is quite possible that he spent much of his theological time in the Gospel of St. John where we read, *"in the beginning was the Word and the Word was with God. He was in the beginning with God. All things were made through Him, and without Him nothing was made that was made. In Him was life and the life was the light of men".*[56] St. John emphasized the divinity of Jesus Christ while the other three apostles of St. Matthew, St. Mark, and St. Luke wrote gospels called *Synoptic Gospels*[57] and emphasized the humanity of Jesus Christ. They are

---

[56] ESV Study Bible. (2008). *EVS Study Bible English Standard Version*. Crossway Bibles. A publishing ministry of Good News Publishers. Wheaton, Illinois. St. John. The Gospel according to John 1:1-4. Page 2017.

[57] Synoptic Gospels. (1976). *A History of Christianity by Paul Johnson*. A Touchstone Book. Published by Simon & Schuster. 2005 Border Books. New York, New York. Page 20.

called Synoptic Gospels because of their commonality of language, order, and subject matter.

Although Martin Luther's commentaries on the Pauline Epistles are famous, it is easy to see why Martin Luther gravitated to the Gospel of John for Christ called John the Apostle whom he loved.[58] There are three references to this in the Scriptures and they are all found in the Gospel of John. Those references are John 19:26 "*...and the disciple whom He loved*"; John 21:7 "*therefore that disciple whom Jesus loved*"; and John 21:20[59]. In John 21:20, we read, "*Peter turned and saw that the disciple whom Jesus loved was following them*". Perhaps it was this type of love by Christ for His Apostle John that Martin Luther wanted from his father since it was largely reported that their relationship was strained and at the least missing the bond of love between a father and a son. It is reported that Luther's father was disappointed that he gave up a promising and lucrative career in law to become a monk in an Augustinian monastery in Wittenberg, Germany. Luther failed to understand that God is the ultimate example of a loving father. His earthly father's failure to love his son as his Heavenly Father loved him gave Luther a distorted view of fatherhood. While it may be unfair to discuss Martin Luther's psychological nature, it is no secret that much has been written about it to totally ignore it, and it does hint of the condition he was in when he lead a revolution.

As an historical footnote, St. John wrote five books of the New Testament. He wrote the Gospel, I John, II John, III John and the book of Revelation, the last book in the Holy Bible. John was the brother of James and they were the sons of Zebedee. They were among the first four Apostles Christ had chosen including brothers (Simon) Peter and Andrew. They were fishermen by trade.

---

[58] ESV Study Bible. (2008). *EVS Study Bible English Standard Version.* Crossway Bibles. A publishing ministry of Good News Publishers. Wheaton, Illinois. St. John. The Gospel according to John 21:20. Page 2072.

[59] Disciple's Study Bible. (1988). The Disciple's Study Bible. *Disciple's Study Bible New International Version.* Holman Bible Publishers. A Cornerstone Bible. Nashville, Tennessee. The New Testament. St. John. The Gospel according to John 21:20. Page 1356.

Finally, I commend a book that sheds light on the Jewish and Christian historical record because it gives us a perspective of tradition and worship and how important is to our Christian psyche. Donna Hobeika Morton, has recently published a book entitled, *Our Jewish Heritage*,[60] which describes the faith of our fathers whose foundations are grounded in the God of Abraham, Isaac and Jacob. Her book offers a good timeline of our historical Christian heritage and how much it is intertwined in the Jewish tradition. I often remind my Christian friends that we happen to worship a Jewish rabbi, Jesus Christ. In her book we can learn about Jesus and His Father who is the best example of a loving father and one that all men should pattern themselves on the virtues of our Heavenly Father. If our Christian denominations adhered to the traditions of the church, and practiced traditional liturgy as it has been celebrated over the last five hundred years, we would not be in the trouble we are in today.

---

[60] Our Jewish Heritage. (2011). *Our Jewish Heritage.* Endorsed by Sid Roth. Donna Hobeika Morton. www.xulonpress.com. Pages 105-181.

Chapter Three

Foundations of Faith

"Trust in the Lord with all thine heart; and lean not unto thine own understanding. In all thy ways acknowledge Him and He shall direct thy paths".[61]

Symbolically, we find that the structure of our faith is grounded in our foundations. Our symbols are vitally important and should not be dismissed so easily. Our houses of worship impact how we conduct services and therefore reflect our approach to worship. For instance, the architectural arrangements of many non-liturgical protestant denominations focus around the pulpit where we find the congregation seated on one side and the choir seated on the other side bearing down on the pulpit where the word is preached. This tends to focus everyone's attention on the minister instead of on the cross. The presence of an altar and cross on the east wall is indicative of a traditional liturgical churches' architecture.

Conversely, in the traditional architectural arrangement in most liturgical churches we find that they are designed based in the shape of a cross. In this configuration one will find a nave in the center accompanied by left and right transepts on the north and the south locations while an altar is found at the head on the

---

[61] Holy Bible, The. (2004). The Holy Bible. *The Holy Bible Authorized King James Version.* World Publishing. Nashville, Tennessee. www.worldpublishing.com. The Old Testament. King Solomon. The Book of Proverbs. 3:5-6. Page 291.

east side. A center aisle has been designed for processionals and recessionals. This center aisle is also called Jacobs Ladder[62] for not only does it transcend the center of the sanctuary but it rises upward toward the altar and the cross which on the eastern wall. It was in Jacob's dream and is proverbially considered the Gateway to Heaven. The focus then, in a liturgical service is on the cross at the altar not on the pulpit. Sometimes the cross has a figure of Christ attached to it and it is then called a crucifix. The absence of a Christ figure on a cross is symbolic of a risen Christ. The cross is there in observance of Christ's sacrifice and the penitential nature of the sanctuary rather than a center pulpit where the word is preached by the protestant minister. If and when a crucifix is present gives us a vivid impression of Jesus' crucifixion and reminds us of the great sacrifice He gave to save us from our sins. I believe churches have erred by not maintaining this architectural symbol in the sanctuary depicting the innocent Christ giving His life as a propitiation for our sins. Again, the cross without the symbol of Christ figure attached to it (crucifix) represents the risen Lord Jesus.

In the traditional liturgical church we find that the pulpit is not at the center or encircled. Indeed, it is at the side because it shares in the service of both the word and the sacrament. Many Christians are seeking the unadulterated "real" substance of God's Word rather than the "processed" substance that many ministers are preaching today. And those seeking the truth are also looking for a real communion with God that can only be attained by participation in the Holy Sacraments especially the sacrament of the Holy Eucharist or Holy Communion. In my humble opinion, aside from man's birth and death experiences, and the experience of Holy Baptism, which are one time physical events, participation in the Holy Eucharist is the most intimate spiritual event man can have with God, our Creator on this earth. Interestingly, we participate in this practice corporately not individually.

---

[62] Believer's Study Bible, The. (1991). The Believer's Study Bible. *The Believer's Study Bible New King James Version.* Thomas Nelson Publishers. Nashville, Tennessee. *Gateway to Heaven.* The Old Testament. Moses. The Book of Genesis 28:10-12. Page 47.

Consequently, the Muslim gentleman who I mentioned in the first short story, *The Scope of the Battlefield*, and I parted ways agreeing to disagree after about an hour of theological debate. This moment seared in me a mission to which I have since been dedicated. It has developed in me for years and was accelerated when I finally decided to put a hold on everything I was involved in at the time and decided to go forward and enter seminary to take graduate theological classes.

Along the way, I was asked by my vicar at the time, Father David Stricker, an Episcopal priest and former United States Army Chaplain, now retired, to lead a new men's prayer group at St. Barnabas'[63] Episcopal Church in Dillon, South Carolina. I suggested to Father David that perhaps there were more qualified men to lead a prayer group and he answered that it may be so, but there were none who were more willing. Maybe he saw something in me or my character that I did not see. Soon thereafter we became organized and I assumed responsibilities as Chapter President and began my tenure as leader of this men's prayer group called the Brotherhood of St. Andrew[64]. It is a national group of Christian men who organized in 1883 at St. James Episcopal Church in Chicago, Illinois. The mission statement of St. Andrews is to instruct men in mentoring skills for young men in the disciplines of daily prayer, regular study and continuous service.

I would be remiss if I did not mention the men in my prayer group who helped me sharpen the tools illustrated in this book and are too important for me not to mention. Their input was invaluable to me as I presided over the discussions and debates we shared over the years. These faithful, dedicated and outstanding Christian men are the Rev. David Stricker, the Rev. H. Fred Gough, my father Paul Hayes, my uncle Elrid Moody, Bill Moody, Royce Cottingham, Ellis Raynor, Warren Mead, Steve Zander,

---

[63] St. Barnabas' Episcopal Church. (1901). *St. Barnabas' Episcopal Church Diocese of South Carolina*. Dillon, South Carolina. www.stbarnabaschurch.org. or www.facebook.com.

[64] Brotherhood of St. Andrew, The. (1883). *The Brotherhood of St. Andrew*. Organized at St. James Episcopal Church in Chicago, Illinois. Ambridge, Pennsylvania. www.brotherhoodofstandrew.org.

F.E. Hobeika, Col. Joe Griffin, Robert Allen, David Hill, J.P. Camp, Chris Corbett and Don Martin.

The Apostle St. Andrew, as you may recall, was the brother of St. Peter. St. Andrew was crucified on an X cross. St. Peter was crucified on an upside down T cross. Our early Christian martyrs lived their faith in Christ knowing they risked their lives for their religious beliefs. It should be noted that nearly all the original twelve Disciples of Christ Jesus died a martyr's[65] death by either spearing, or stoning, or crucifixion, or beheading[66]. The only exceptions were the Apostle Judas who hanged himself after betraying our Lord Jesus Christ and the Apostle John who died of an advanced age but had suffered for years from the results of having been tortured in a vat of boiling oil and somehow survived. His life ended on the Island of Patmos where he wrote his last book, the Book of Revelation, which is also the last book in the New Testament and the Holy Bible. The Apostle John was the disciple that Christ stated on more than one occasion that He loved. This is referenced in the last short story, *A Historical Perspective*.

I often wonder if we have the same level of commitment to our faith as the disciples did as well as the early Christians who died by the thousands and had to go underground to worship freely in the catacombs to keep Christianity alive. And no, they did not have to be tempted to inherit seventy virgins in paradise by committing homicide or suicide and strapping a bomb to their body and killing innocent people. They believed on faith in Jesus Christ and the promise of eternity in heaven with Him, pure and simple. The early Christians lived in fear and yet they still believed. They survived by worshiping in their homes (refer to Colossians 4:15, Philemon 2, Romans 16) to maintain their freedom of worship because they were hunted down by enemies of their religion. Today, we live in a country that practices religious freedom and we are not currently in danger of being put to death for our beliefs like the Jewish and

---

[65] Martyr. (2012) Catholic Online. www.catholic.org/saints/martyr.php

[66] Foxe's Book of Martyrs. (2006). *Foxe's Book of Martyrs A History of The Lives, Sufferings, and Triumphant Deaths of the Early Christian and Protestant Martyrs*. Edited by William Byron Forbush, D.D. Faithpoint Press. Produced by Cliff Road Books. Pages 14-17.

Christian people of Europe just a century ago, yet we hardly attend church or practice any form of religious worship on a regular basis.

Some say that we should be careful for this could very likely change in the future. Already there is a federal law[67] that was passed by the United States Congress that could be used as it has been in other countries to mute Christian religious thoughts not actions and place clergy in the category of being guilty of hate crimes. Tolerance of Judeo-Christian beliefs has been eroding in America and around the world for some time now, yet it seems tolerance of other religions gets a free pass. Indeed, there are reports around the world of Christian missionaries who are martyred for their beliefs numbering in the hundreds every year.

It was in the ministry of prayer and Bible study that the concept of this book came to mind and gained its footing. The title, *Pentagon of Faith Sacred Theism vs. Secular Humanism A Christian's Need for the Traditional Faith of our Fathers*, was chosen because we live in a challenging world of spiritual warfare. We are fighting for the souls of the lost daily. Since I have a military background, I have likened this book to an army field manual. In it are the five Christian faith foundations useful to combat the evil that surrounds us. It may come as no surprise to some that our battle is both internal and external. We all know it is external but to underscore the internal nature of our ranks being compromised I refer to the Gospel of Mark where we read, *"the people were astonished at his teaching, for he taught them as one having authority and not as the scribes. In their synagogue was a man with an unclean spirit; he cried out, 'what have you to do with us, Jesus of Nazareth? Have you come to destroy us? I know who you are—the Holy One of God!'"*[68] This is evidence of betrayers in our ranks and should give us pause when we think of changing or modifying our traditional ways of worship.

---

[67] U.S. Federal Law. (2009) Hate Crimes Legislation (18 U.S.C.@2). Dr. James Dobson. A Focus on the Family Affiliate. Colorado Springs, Colorado. www.citizenlink.org.

[68] Catholic Study Bible, The. (1990). The Catholic Study Bible. *The Catholic Study Bible New American Bible*. Oxford University Press, Inc. The New Testament. St. Mark. The Gospel according to Mark 1:22-24. New York, New York. Page 69.

Chapter Four

Our Common Enemy

"Be not wise in thine own eyes: fear the Lord, and depart from evil. It shall be health to thy navel and marrow to thy bones". [69]

I recently received an email and then later saw in print an article entitled, *Shrinking Jesus and Betraying the Faith*[70] from the retired Bishop of South Carolina, the Rt. Rev. C. Fitzsimmons Allison, who made some incisive and useful comments on the depth of the cauldron where we modern Christians reside. The following excerpts are herein provided to underscore the predicament in which we find ourselves in today and it is not limited to any particular denomination. Indeed all denominations are facing this heresy in their ranks at some level, some to greater degrees than others. A selection from the article follows:

> *"Christian faith, but not secular faith, now effectively banned from schools, colleges, and universities, has been relegated to the private and subjective arena. The result is the growing*

---

[69] Holy Bible, The. (2004). The Holy Bible. *The Holy Bible Authorized King James Version.* World Publishing. Nashville, Tennessee. www.worldpublishing.com. The Old Testament. King Solomon. The Book of Proverbs 3:7-8. Page 291.

[70] Jubilate Deo, Winter 2012. Volume 116, No. 3. (2012). The Episcopal Diocese of South Carolina. Rt. Rev. C. Fitzsimmons Allison, XII Bishop of South Carolina. Page 1.

popularity of any who eliminate from Christian faith all that secular trust finds incompatible: miracles, the radical nature of sin and the consequent radical nature of grace, transcendence, holiness, and our human desperate need for God's initiative action in Jesus...Doctrine is 'that which is taught, what is held, put forth as true' (Webster).

Doctrine is a synonym for teaching, when we 'do not readily think in terms of Doctrine' we are unaware and ignorant of Christian teaching. This is true of both 'liberals' and 'conservatives'. We were warned in Scripture about losing our grasp on doctrine and the danger of false doctrine; ('...so that we may no longer be children, tossed to and fro and carried about with every wind of doctrine by cunning men, by their craftiness in deceitful wiles.' Ephesians 4:14, (see also Titus 2:7, I Timothy 1:3 and 4:16, II John 10, II Timothy 3:16, 4:2). Christian doctrine...has been replaced by the doctrines of litigation, abortion, divorce, sexual behavior outside of marriage and all kinds of current politically correct doctrines, as well as teachings that Jesus is reduced from the Son of God to a 'subversive sage'."

And I might add the false doctrines of idolatry and greed. The term "subversive sage"[71] according to Bishop Allison is referenced in the article from books by two contemporary theologians, Marcus Borg and John Dominic Crossan. They consider Jesus no

---

[71] Meeting Jesus Again for the First Time. (1995). *Meeting Jesus Again for the First Time The Historical Jesus & The Heart of Contemporary Faith.* Marcus J. Borg. Harper San Francisco. A Division of Harper Collins Publishers. New York, New York. Page 119.

more divine than Mahatma Gandhi[72] or civil rights leader Martin Luther King[73]. They describe with their jaundiced view a Jesus who was nothing more than a "spiritual person", or "a mediator of the sacred", or a "shaman"[74] or one of those persons like Abraham, Moses, Buddha, Muhammad and the like. There is a current trend which calls us not to identify a name with the responsible evil. This thinking considers that if it has no name, no one can rise up against it. Evil, sin and false gods are not always found just in the external or opposing religions. Many times we are fighting an internal battle. There are dozens of well meaning people who attend church but they tread on false theology or outright apostasy in what they believe. Faith-based theological doctrine is being replaced by self-esteem based psychology. Satan and sin are no longer the enemy nor are they regularly mentioned in our churches. Satan has been reinvented by the elite secular humanists of our society as nothing other than a little troublemaker who is of no consequence to us since he presents us no harm or danger. On the other hand, Christian symbols such as the cross are being replaced by worldly symbols such as a large globe of the world in our churches and seminaries.

An example of the internal battle of false doctrine is one I succumbed to in my twenties. It is a doctrine of 'once saved always saved'. This may be true but it is a half truth. Those who live by it choose a wayward life thinking they can posses a sinful nature and get away with their transgressions because they have a trump card in their hip pocket that they will pull out on judgment day and slip through the gates of heaven. They believe falsely that they can live for themselves, that they have no need of repentance, and that their sins will be automatically forgiven. They believe they

---

[72] Gandhi, Mahatma. (1948). Encyclopedia Britannica. *Encyclopedia Britannica 2009 Deluxe Edition.* Chicago: Encyclopedia Britannica.

[73] King, Martin Luther. (2001). Random House College Dictionary. *Random House Webster's College Dictionary 2nd Revised and Updated Edition.* Random House, Inc. New York, New York. www.randomhouse.com. Page 731.

[74] Meeting Jesus Again for the First Time. (1995). Marcus J. Borg. Harper San Francisco. A Division of Harper Collins Publishers. New York, New York. Page 32.

cannot "lose their religion". What they have failed to learn is that living a Christian life comes with a price. Our behavior and how we conduct ourselves matters to God. If we do not abide by Christ's teachings like the lessons he taught us in the Sermon on the Plain[75] and the Sermon on the Mount[76] which includes the Beatitudes, then "once saved always saved" is only partially true. The second half of this passage which most people ignore is that we must repent, turn away from our selfish desires and lead new lives following the commandments of God and not repeating our past sins. When we were baptized, we received the Holy Spirit who came to dwell in us, but we also accepted an obligation to obey. As baptized Christians, we are to become new creatures where the old self, the sinful self, is cast away. "Once saved, always saved" is true as long as we turn our lives around and abide by the Holy Scriptures. When we are baptized we are not granted a 'get out of jail' or 'just visiting pass' as if we were playing the board game Monopoly."[77] We must abide by the whole body of this doctrine not just half of it. Certainly, we will fail at this because we are human and therefore not perfect, but our conviction and aim should be to live for Christ.

There is another dangerous theology or internal battle that has taken hold in our Christian churches. It is a material based theology and probably one of the most destructive and fearful. It is sometimes referred to as prosperity theology. It links the level of our faith to the level of our possessions. In other words, if we are faithful, then we will have many possessions or if we are not faithful then we will have very little in terms of worldly possessions. For those Christians who subscribe to this theology I recommend that you read Jesus' parable of Lazarus and the rich man found in

---

[75] Thompson Chain-Reference Bible. (2009). *Thompson Chain-Reference Bible King James Version*. B.B. Kirkbride Bible Co., Inc. Indianapolis, Indiana. The New Testament. St. Luke. The Gospel according to Luke 6:17-49. Pages 1086-1087.

[76] Thompson Chain-Reference Bible. (2009). *Thompson Chain-Reference Bible King James Version*. B.B. Kirkbride Bible Co., Inc. Indianapolis, Indiana. The New Testament. St. Matthew. The Gospel according to Matthew 5:1-11. Page 1017.

[77] Monopoly. (1904). Popular Board Game of Chance. Parker Brothers.

the Gospel of St. Luke chapter 16 verses 19-31. God provides our material need. What God provides in abundance is in the area of love, kindness, gentleness, righteousness, meekness, charity and so on. He does not provide more clothes, shoes, toys, cars, boats, houses, and so on that we do not need. When we tread on this material venue, we find ourselves in a precarious condition.

Jesus' parable about the ten virgins[78] where five of the ten had their oil lamps filled when the Master came, while the lamps of the other five virgins' oil lamps were empty, is a testament to the above apostasy. The parable of the ten virgins is supported in Matthew 7:21 where it is written, "Not everyone who says to me, 'Lord, Lord,' shall enter the kingdom of heaven, but he who does the will of My Father in heaven. Many will say to me in that Day, 'Lord, Lord, have we not prophesied in your name, cast out demons in your name, and done wonders in your name?' And Then I will declare to them, 'I never knew you; depart from me, you who practice lawlessness.'"[79] Therefore, if we abide by our Lord's teachings, we will join Him in glory and receive our reward in heaven. If not, we will continue to live in death and destruction and surely go to hell. One might ask then, "How can a benevolent and compassionate God condemn me to hell"? Well, God is benevolent and He is compassionate. He gave us not only our free will to choose Him, but He gave us His only begotten Son to die on the Cross to save us from our sins. If we reject His Son, Jesus, and do not abide by the lessons He taught us in the Holy Scriptures, then we exercise our free will and choose to condemn ourselves.

Another internal battle of questionable doctrine is based on the verse found in the Gospel of St. Luke where we read, "glory to

---

[78] Believer's Study Bible, The. (1991). The Believer's Study Bible. *The Believer's Study Bible New King James Version*. Thomas Nelson Publishers. Nashville, Tennessee. The New Testament. St. Matthew. The Gospel according to Matthew 25:1-13. Pages 1381-1382.

[79] Believer's Study Bible, The. (1991). The Believer's Study Bible. *The Believer's Study Bible New King James Version*. Thomas Nelson Publishers. Nashville, Tennessee. The New Testament. St. Matthew. The Gospel according to Matthew 7:21-23. Page 1348.

God in the highest and peace on earth and good will toward men".[80] The ending to this verse is translated in Greek as, ευνδοκιvαß, meaning "of good will". Early Christian translators interpreted this in the nominative case while most modern translators interpret this in the genitive case. The entire translation changes on one word when we learn from the modern translator that this statement is not meant for all mankind. In other words, the peace that the angels sang that belonged to the earth as a result of Christ's birth is not a generic, worldwide peace for all mankind, but a peace limited to those who obtain favor with God by believing in His Son Jesus.[81] This statement is supported in St. Paul's Epistle to the Romans which says:

> *"Therefore, since we have been justified by faith, we have peace through our Lord Jesus Christ. Through Him we have also obtained access by faith in this grace in which we stand, and we rejoice in hope of the glory of God. More than that, we rejoice in our hope of the glory of God. More than that, we rejoice in our sufferings, knowing that suffering produces endurance, and endurance produces character, and character produces hope, and hope does not put us to shame, because God's love had been poured into our hearts through the Holy Spirit which has been given to us".[82]*

---

[80] Thompson Chain-Reference Bible. (2007). *Thompson Chain-Reference Bible King James Version*. B.B. Kirkbride Bible Company, Inc. Indianapolis, Indiana. The New Testament. St. Luke. The Gospel according to Luke 2:14. Page 1080.

[81] Basics of Biblical Greek. (1999). *Basics of Biblical Greek Grammar*. Zondervan Publishing House. Grand Rapids, Michigan. Mounce, William D. Page 45.

[82] MacArthur Study Bible, The. (2010). The MacArthur Study Bible. *The MacArthur Study Bible English Standard Version*. Crossway. A publishing ministry of Good News Publishers. The New Testament. St. Paul. The Letter of Paul to the Romans 5:1-5. Pages 1656-1657. www.ESVBIBLE.org.

Walt Kelly, creator of the Pogo[83] strip once said, "We have met the enemy, and he is us". It would be too easy to point fingers at all things around us and claim it or they are the reason for our failure to remain true to the traditional faith of our fathers. Finger pointing and demonizing are tactics used by the enemies of sacred theism. We should not acquiesce and use the tools of our enemies for then we may become like them. Our generation has reached a point in its behavior where finger pointing and not taking responsibility for our actions has become nearly a sport and certainly there are children of the dark who are better at it than the children of the light. But if we were to shirk the blame for the condition we find ourselves, then have we become our friend or our foe? It is not only our necessity but our obligation to accept blame for our shortcomings and failures. If we, by omission or commission are at fault, then we need to take personal responsibility for our situation because it is the first step to correcting our course. In modern business terms, we are taking ownership of our transgressions and we will hold ourselves accountable and responsible for those actions known and unknown because as it was in the traditional faith of our father to "do right thing". In other words, if we sin, we should be held accountable and not give reason for our sins on anything but our own advice. We are all guilty of allowing secular humanism to invade our institutions and it has taken hold in our thinking and changed our values and consequently modified our beliefs.

Many years ago after World War II, there was a concern that communism which is a political economic system that functions in contrast to capitalism[84], a market based economic system, would take over the world. A term was coined known as 'creeping

---

[83] The Best of Pogo. (1982). *The Best of Pogo Edited by Mrs. Walt Kelly and Bill Crouch, Jr.* A Fireside Book. Simon & Schuster Publishers. New York, New York. www.igopogo.com.

[84] Capitalism. (2001). Random House College Dictionary. *Random House Webster's College Dictionary 2nd Revised and Updated Edition*. Random House, Inc. New York, New York. www.randomhousewords.com. Page 198.

communism."[85] The term "creeping" can be applied to our present state in the Christian faith. We have maintained a vigilance abroad looking at the transgressions of others and under the radar and yet in plain sight we have allowed "creeping secular humanism" to take hold of our institutions and infiltrate our minds. In a sense, our pickets have fallen asleep at our gates. Or, another way to say it, in a classical sense, we have allowed a Trojan horse[86] into our cities or in this case our minds. This scenario is referred to in the *Iliad* by Homer,[87] an 8th century B.C. Greek poet who wrote the epic poems, the Iliad and the Odyssey. It is a tale by Virgil, a 1st century B.C. Latin poet who wrote in the *Aeneid* about the Trojan War and how the Greeks finally entered the city of Troy, hidden inside a wooden horse, and overwhelmed their enemy. Metaphorically it means any strategy that deceives an enemy and enters into its fortified space.

As creeping secular humanism slowly began to dismantle our educational institutions to gain its footing; once it established a foundation it then began chipping away at our political institutions, then our judicial institutions fell to its persuasive power, and finally our religious institutions fell victim; and now we have opened ourselves to compromise where tolerance is the norm and conviction is a long forgotten virtue. My friend Tom Moore of Aiken, South Carolina by way of James Island, South Carolina and Washington, D.C. said to me one time that he interpreted tolerance as "a person, who stood for nothing at all, or one who had no convictions, or one who lives with no principles". I believe he is right. If we do not stand for anything, then we are defeated.

---

[85] Communism. (1976). *A History of Christianity.* A Touchstone Book. Published by Simon & Schuster. New York, New York. Paul Johnson. Page 492.

[86] Trojan Horse. (2002). Random House College Dictionary. *Random House College Dictionary 2nd Revised and Updated Edition.* Random House, Inc. New York, New York. www.randomhouse.com. Page 1401.

[87] Homer. (2001). The American Heritage College Dictionary. *The American Heritage College Dictionary Fourth Edition.* Joseph P. Pickett, Vice President and Executive Editor. Published by the Houghton Mifflin Company. Boston, Massachusetts. Page 663.

Socialism has without a doubt its roots in the secular humanism. A socialist[88] socialist is one who believes in the common ownership of property for the benefit of the masses. A byproduct of socialism is the erosion of personal freedom. These personal freedoms include the freedom of speech, freedom of religion, freedom to congregate, freedom to protest, freedom of the press, freedom to bear arms and many other freedoms that the United States Constitution was written to protect our citizenry from tyranny. The pendulum has swung too far in the direction of the loss of personal freedom and there is a profound need to bring it back to the center and at least leaning toward the values and beliefs of sacred theism. Much has been written about secular humanism and its promotion of the self as the center of the universe but no one has developed sacred deism as a unit until now.

Sacred theism was first alluded to in *The Scope of the Battlefield,* but it is a new term that requires additional explanation. Sacred theism is the condition wherein God is at the center of the universe, not man. It recognizes that there is one God who is creator of the universe. He is the one God who is omnipotent, omnipresent, and omniscient. He is the one God who is our Heavenly Father which means He is not our Heavenly *Mother*. He is not kin to Mother Earth which is a pagan symbol to counterweigh the deity and divinity of God and promote pantheism[89] wherein its roots are planted. Sacred theism is a belief in one God who made man in His image. He is the one and only Theos, and He is Sacred. Sacred theism requires that we show reverence to Him, our only Creator, and that we also fear Him which is defined as showing Him reverence and respect. It is in this fear that we come to understand Him and respect Him.

---

[88] Socialist. (2002). The American Heritage College Dictionary. *The American Heritage College Dictionary Fourth Edition.* Joseph P. Pickett, Vice President and Executive Editor. Published by the Houghton Mifflin Company. Boston, Massachusetts. Page 1314.

[89] Pantheism. (2002). The American heritage College Dictionary. *The American Heritage College Dictionary Fourth Edition.* Joseph P. Pickett, Vice President and Executive Editor. Published by the Houghton Mifflin Company. Boston, Massachusetts. Page 1006.

When we do this we learn to worship and praise Him which is the sole purpose of man's creation.

Our common enemy is all around us in our homes, our schools, our shopping places, our places of worship, and our military services to name a few. There is no safe haven where we can go to avoid the enemy. In other words, our enemy is everywhere even at times in the mirror. We should take heed to the words in the Epistle of St. Paul to the Romans 1:18-32 when we allow secular humanism to take hold in our lives. In the New International Version of Romans we read,

> *"The wrath of God is being revealed from heaven against all the godlessness and wickedness of men who suppress the truth by their wickedness, since what may be known about God is plain to them, because God has made it plain to them. For since the creation of the world God's invisible qualities—his eternal power and divine nature— have been clearly seen, being understood from what has been made, so that men are without excuse. For although they knew God, they neither glorified him as God nor gave thanks to him, but their thinking became futile and their foolish hearts were darkened. Although they claimed to be wise, they became fools and exchanged the glory of the immortal God for images made to look like mortal man and birds and animals and reptiles. Therefore God gave them over in the sinful desires of their hearts to sexual impurity for the degrading of their bodies with one another. They exchanged the truth of God for a lie, and worshipped and served created things rather than the Creator—who is forever praised. Because of this, God gave them over to shameful lusts. Even their women exchanged natural relations for unnatural ones. In the same*

way the men also abandoned natural relations with women and were inflamed with lust for one another. Men committed indecent acts with other men, and received in themselves the due penalty for their perversion. Furthermore, since they did not think it worthwhile to retain the knowledge of God, he gave them over to a depraved mind; to do what ought not to be done. They have become filled with every kind of wickedness, evil, greed and depravity. They are full of envy, murder, strife, deceit and malice. They are gossips, slanderers, God-haters, insolent, arrogant and boastful; they invent ways of doing evil; they disobey their parents; they are senseless, faithless, heartless, and ruthless. Although they know God's righteous decree that those who do such things deserve death, they not only continue to do these very things but also approve of those who practice them".

So we should constantly be on our guard. We should prepare ourselves and protect ourselves with regular study of the Scriptures. A daily devotion and Bible study are great sources to help us build a fortress around us to protect us from the enemy. Consequently, the evolution of the points in this book was discussed and debated in regular Bible study with the men of St. Barnabas' Episcopal Church's Brotherhood of St. Andrew. We have been meeting and studying together over the last several years and their names are mentioned in the previous section, Chapter Three. We did not always agree but together we shared a bond of discipleship and support of and for each other. We are brothers in Christ in whom we love. I count them as critical for the contributions they made in word and spirit while discussing the true doctrines of the church and the principles on which we stand.

Chapter Five

Why We Believe

"Honour the Lord with thy substance, and with thy first fruits of all thine increase: So shall thy barns be filled with plenty, and thy presses shall burst out with new wine".[90]

Christians around the world are yearning for God's Word and a return to the practices and traditions of sacred theism and away from the immorality and paganism of secular humanism. In recent decades ministers have not necessarily been good teachers. This sounds like a critical statement but here is why this statement is included in this chapter. There are many forces working against the people of God. Perhaps that is why at a recent clerical conference hosted by my dear friend Dr. Beverly Jessup, Director of the Chaplains' department at First Health hospital in Pinehurst, North Carolina; participants in our group were informed that literally hundreds of ordained ministers leave the ranks of the clergy for a different vocation every year. And I am sure if we analyze the data; we will see that many left for teaching or staff positions with benefits. Others may have left because they lost interest in God's ministry. Still others may have left for better pay and benefits. There are an unlimited number of reasons why men and women (some

---

[90] Holy Bible, The. (2004). The Holy Bible. *The Holy Bible Authorized King James Version.* World Publishing. Nashville, Tennessee. www.worldpublishing.com. The Old Testament. King Solomon. The Book of Proverbs 3:9-10. Page 291.

denominations endorse women for the clergy) leave the ministry for new vocations. However, I believe that the highest percentage of clergy leave because of burnout. They find over the years they cannot fulfill the demands of the job. One of the hardest lessons to learn in the life of a minister is to say no. Therefore, the ordained ministry is not for the faint of heart.

Often ministers feel that they are a targets of society and certainly we are looked at with a great degree of trepidation and probably more so than others in different professions. It takes a person who is somewhat thick skinned to survive year in and year out in full time ministry and quite frankly if they are to survive they need to have a bit of narcissism in their blood. If we are not being verbally attacked from the outside then we are being brutally challenged from the inside. It takes years of training to develop a good minister. It is not for everyone but it does have its rewards. Ministers like teachers are held to higher standards of accountability than other professions. The Apostle St. James writes is his New Testament book James 3:1, "my brethren, let not many of you become teachers, knowing that we shall receive a stricter judgment". Some say that this means that teachers and preachers are held doubly accountable. This could make many hesitate to enter into either of these professions if we believe St. James's words. We reason that if we are held doubly accountable then we will be doubly rewarded. However, I did not enter the ministry for a reward and I strongly suggest anyone considering a life of ministry for the sake of reward look for another vocation.

Why we believe is dependent on our fear of God. This is not the same fear as being frightened. This is the type of fear that demands respect and honor due His name. There are many references on the fear of God in the Scriptures. For example, we read in Psalm 67:7, "God shall bless us, let all the ends of the earth fear him," and in Proverbs 2:5, "then you will understand the fear of the Lord and find the knowledge of God," and Proverbs 89:6-7, "who among the heavenly beings is like the Lord, a God greatly to be feared in the council of the holy ones, and awesome above all who are around him"? The fear of God requires discipline and discipline sometimes requires punishment. But the Catch 22[91] is that few ministers want to be the disciplinarian or to be the one to cause anyone grief or pain. Better to leave that to the next person or so they think. Again, no one wants to rock the boat. However, if we are disciplined and corrected or punished as needed, we begin to fully understand that there are consequences for our words, actions, and deeds. From these consequences we begin to develop a sense of self-sacrifice and the art of giving and charity follow. We learn that our hope is eternal and not of the things of this world. This is characteristically a hallmark of a Christian because it causes us to develop endurance and endurance gives us character and character gives us hope as the Apostle St. Paul wrote in his epistle to the Romans[92]. When we suffer and through our suffering, we are drawn closer to Jesus Christ because He suffered for us in His life on earth and on the cross. We now understand not only the magnitude of His sacrifice as a propitiation for our sins but also the unlimited and infinite love of a devoted and caring Heavenly Father. God created us for Himself. If we are to be complete we must make God a part of our lives. If we don't, we will never reach our ultimate destination designed especially for us by God. It includes the ultimate peace, joy and happiness that exceed all understanding. This is fundamental for every Christian to understand the principles of a life practicing the disciplines of sacred theism.

    Just think about it for a moment. How often through recorded history has man turned his back on God? How often have you turned your back on God? I know I did in my early twenties and it took me years to crawl out of that hole. I wanted a taste of the world and although it was sweet at first, it was a lifestyle that became bitter as I grew older. I finally climbed out of that dark hole a few

---

[91] Catch 22. (2002). The American Heritage Dictionary. *The American Heritage College Dictionary Fourth Edition.* Joseph P. Pickett, Vice President and Executive Editor. Published by the Houghton Mifflin Company. Boston, Massachusetts. Page 227.

[92] Believer's Study Bible, The. (1991). The Believer's Study Bible. *The Believer's Study Bible New King James Version.* Thomas Nelson Publishers. Nashville, Tennessee. The New Testament. St. Paul. The Epistle of Paul to The Romans 5:1-5. Page 1605.

years ago, but it took a mighty effort over the course of several years to get that lifestyle behind me. I must say that I regret turning my back on God and every day making that conscious decision. They say hindsight is 20/20 and from where I am now, I would never recommend anyone to make that near disastrous decision as I did. To overcome the addictions and secular gravity of this world was not easy. Thank God for His mercy and forgiveness of me.

We do know because it has been recorded from the beginning of time that men have turned their back on God over and over again. Yet, God is still there waiting patiently for us to return to Him. What immeasurable love this is! He wants what is best for us and sometimes He has to allow us to be hurt or to fall down so we can turn our lives around. He encourages us to head up the straight and narrow path that leads to eternity with Him in heaven. Along the way we are constantly being grabbed by what seems to be a magnetic field to fall into temptation. We must depart from temptation and one way to resist it is to recite the Lord's Prayer found in chapter nineteen of this book. It is a great resource of strength and inspiration in our time of trouble. However, Jesus cautions us in a parable of *The Leaven of the Pharisees and Sadducees*[93]. In St. Matthew we read,

> *"When they went across the lake, the disciples forgot to take bread. 'Be careful', Jesus said to them. "Be on your guard against the yeast of the Pharisees and Sadducees.' They discussed this among themselves and said, 'it is because we didn't bring any bread.' Aware of their discussion, Jesus asked, 'You of little faith, why are you talking among yourselves about having no bread?' Do you still not understand? Don't you remember the five loaves of the five thousand*

---

[93] Seasons of Reflection. (1996). *Seasons of Reflection The New International Version Bible in 365 Daily Readings with Special Helps on Prayer*. International Bible Society. Colorado Springs, Colorado. The New Testament. St. Matthew. The Gospel of Matthew 16:5-12. Page 71.

and how many basketfuls you fathered? Or even the seven loaves for the four thousand, and how many basketfuls you fathered? How is it you don't understand that I was not talking to you about bread? But be on your guard against the yeast of the Pharisees and Sadducees, 'Then they understood that he was not telling them to guard against the yeast used in the bread, but against the teaching of the Pharisees and Sadducees.'"

From this passage of Holy Scripture we should come to understand that we are to maintain our vigilance so that we do not become the victim or fall into the trap of false teachings. The temptations of this world seem pleasing to the eye or touch or our senses but they are lures we should avoid or they will become traps that will too often ensnare us. We should keep our eyes on the Lord and He will direct our paths and protect us from all harm and destruction. And in a word, keep our *faith* in God. So, why do we believe? We believe because we love God and desire to keep His commandments.

Chapter Six

Tough and Courageous Love

"My son, despise not the chastening of the Lord: neither be weary of his correction: For whom the Lord loveth he correcteth; even as a father the son in whom he delighteth".[94]

The categories of discipline and punishment; and suffering and pain, are not what ministers want to inflict on their congregations, nor does God. However, it takes great love to discipline a child. And I am not talking about discipline as in verbal or physical abuse. Abuse is not discipline and is not a part of these previously mentioned categories. Discipline is defined as how and when you admonish and instruct a child or brother or sister out of love; not by frustration or anger but lovingly and caringly. Unfortunately, the theological development for many Christians is on the level of a child and many grow into adulthood still suckling on mother's milk. It is my opinion that the root cause of this lack of theological development in many adult Christians is the lack of discipline in their developing years as a child or young adult. There is no other place to point to for this shortfall. We are not

---

[94] Holy Bible, The. (2004). The Holy Bible. *The Holy Bible Authorized King James Version.* World Publishing. Nashville, Tennessee. www.worldpublishing.com. The Old Testament. King Solomon. The Book of Proverbs 3:11-12. Page 291.

going to play the blame game that the world of secular humanism plays. There is an age of accountability. Even our laws deem that to there is an age where our parents are no longer responsible for our actions. We are directed by Scripture when we live by the precepts of sacred theism to admonish our brothers and sisters in Christ when they do wrong. When it is done correctly and the receiver realizes it is done for their best interest, then we succeed. If we admonish wrongly, then we cause the child or young adult to rebel. The best gauge is to discipline out of love and in most cases we will succeed.

Children, when punished out of love, do not have any other place to go or retreat outside of their home. Unfortunately, if they are old enough they become runaways and end up on the streets and in the world of vice. Adults, when they are admonished out of brotherly or sisterly love, are able to go elsewhere and many times choose to leave their congregation for another church congregation that agrees with their views. This is one reason we find new churches being established on a regular basis. In these cases, if the disagreement becomes public, members will take one side or another. And often this causes a rift or split. If the split is made for theological reasons, it is justified but for any other reason it is subject to debate. And this is the risk all ministers face. It is not a surprise for many that this situation was predicted in Scripture. In the latter days, hearers of the message want their ears tickled not scratched. For it is written in II Timothy;

> *"For the time will come when men will not put up with sound doctrine. Instead, to suit their own desires, they will gather around them a great number of teachers to say what their itching ears want to hear. They will turn their ears away from the truth and turn aside to myths".*[95]

---

[95] Disciples Study Bible, The. (1988). The Disciple's Study Bible. *The Disciple's Study Bible New International Version.* Holman Bible Publishers. A Cornerstone Bible. Nashville, Tennessee. The New Testament. St. Paul. The second Epistle of Paul to Timothy 4:3-4. Page 1559.

Therefore, we have a Scripture foundation, wherein we can interpret and understand why secular humanism is wrought with error and mysticism. Remember how we discussed earlier in the short story of the *Foundations of Faith*, that our societal institutions would be compromised, such as the institution of government. Now, add to the equation the reality of a hostile US Department of Justice, and the threat of litigation and even of incarceration under the current "Hate Crimes Law". And we wonder why parishioners are not hearing the truth of the Gospel of Jesus Christ. Some ministers are timid and afraid to proclaim the whole truth of the Gospel for fear of this kind of reprisal, not to mention the reprisal from inside their ranks. Today, some ministers are told to be inclusive and tolerant facing many views and beliefs. Many ministers are being encouraged or persuaded to teach every view or belief except the truth and values of Christianity. They are being threatened with the loss of a job, or even the possibility of being incarcerated while facing criminal charges for proclaiming the Word of God. Perhaps now, one can see why the truth of the Word of God has become so diluted. It requires great courage from the clergy to deliver the truth of God's unfiltered Word. I liken today's period in Church history to the early years of Christianity when the first believers had to go underground to practice their beliefs. It is a real issue for Christians today and it requires a true reality check if we are to choose to accept the terms of our faith and live by those disciplines and beliefs.

The multitude of Christian brands has further diluted the message and with so many choices and voices, no wonder people are confused and lost. Many ministers find themselves in a paradox such as the proverbial dilemma known as "between the rock and hard place" or "between the devil and the deep blue sea". In either case it is not a good place to be. It seems that ministers, who teach the plain and unadulterated truth of the Gospel, often lose followers who are looking for a passive God who is never angered by their sinful ways (they think) and thus face no penalty for their sin. On the other hand, ministers who teach only of a benevolent, passive and loving God seem to keep their houses of worship filled to the brim; the offering plate is over-flowing and there is plenty of food on the table, so to speak. The sad part of this equation is that from this second table, no hunger or thirst can be quenched, so it must have unlimited amounts of food to keep people coming back. This proverbial table may contain whole food that quenches the hunger in the flesh (secular humanism) but what it needs is soul food that quenches the hunger in the spirit (sacred theism).

Christians need a good helping of the fear of God. The God of Abraham, Isaac and Jacob is real and He is engaged and He wants to be an active participant in our lives. We cannot fear Him if we are not taught to fear Him. We learn that when we are disciplined as a child. The fear of God is the beginning of holiness and righteousness. We need to know that there are severe consequences when we do not obey God. Look what happened to *Sodom and Gomorrah*[96] or the *Great Flood*[97]. Our place in eternity depends on it. In the Old Testament book of Malachi, we read, "then those who feared the Lord talked with each other, and the Lord listened and heard. A scroll of remembrance was written in His presence concerning those who feared the Lord and honored His name".[98]

The fruit of this orchard in our journey is compiled in this book. I believe it is a must reading for any thoughtful or serious Christian. After you read this book, and hopefully thereafter, when you are asked, "Why are you a Christian"? You may easily respond to that question by what you have learned from the lessons found in this book. I hope you will respond with this assertion, "I am a

---

[96] Catholic Study Bible, The. (1990). The Catholic Study Bible. *The Catholic Study Bible New American Bible.* Oxford University Press, Inc. New York, New York. The Old Testament. Moses. The Pentateuch. The Book of Genesis Chapter 19. Pages 22-23.

[97] Catholic Study Bible, The. (1990). The Catholic Study Bible. *The Catholic Study Bible New American Bible.* Oxford University Press, Inc. New York, New York. The Old Testament. Moses. The Pentateuch. The Book of Genesis Chapters 6-9. Pages 10-13.

[98] Disciple's Study Bible, The. (1988). The Disciple's Study Bible. *The Disciple's Study Bible New International Version.* Holman Bible Publishers. A Cornerstone Bible. Nashville, Tennessee. The Old Testament. Malachi. The Book of Malachi 3:16. Pages 1160-1161.

Christian because of Jesus Christ, the only Son of the one living God, who died on the Cross at Calvary to save me from my sins. My life has changed for the better when I repented of my sins and received Him into my life. I have departed from my wayward ways and I began my walk in His holy ways following His commandments".

    I count this book as necessary for any Christian or theological student and hope it will also be a good companion for your Holy Bible. It provides more than just the good earthly food from the table that feeds our flesh. It provides the concise spiritual food which we have been missing recently that comes from the altar of God. This book is written to develop and contrast the warring sides of secular humanism and sacred theism. These opposing sides are like oil and water; they do not mix. This book identifies the theological problems as real or perceived as well as references them and it gives solutions for treating the same. It is written to reacquaint the reader with our Christian roots and the foundations which have largely been forgotten, dismissed or misunderstood. This book's simplicity underscores precisely why it was written for the new Christian and the wayward Christian who has a desire to reestablish their fellowship with the Christian church and their Creator and One God. Each chapter will begin with the summary for quick and easy reference. The summary will be followed by an exposition that will develop into further detail the subject matter. I pray you will enjoy reading this book and that you will be blessed by its lessons.

Chapter Seven

The Raging Battle

"Happy is the man that findeth wisdom, and the man that getteth understanding. For the merchandise of it is better than the merchandise of silver and the gain thereof than fine gold. She is more precious than rubies; and all these things thou canst desire are not to be compared unto her. Length of days is in her right hand; and in her left hand riches and honour. Her ways are ways of pleasantness, and all her paths are peace. She is a tree of life to them that lay hold upon her; and happy is every one that retaineth her".[99]

This religious field manual is written as an aid to the Christians who feel that something is missing in their spiritual journey as we navigate the battlefield that is strewn with remnants of our sacred theism past and which has been chewed up by the evil forces of secular humanism. Our once proud Christian nation is rapidly becoming a hodgepodge of multiple gods. We are in the midst of an ongoing spiritual warfare and the battle is over the hearts and minds of all believers. One of my seminary classes included lessons on exorcism or casting out demons, a necessity that is not taught

---

[99] Holy Bible, The. (2004). The Holy Bible. *The Holy Bible Authorized King James Version.* World Publishing. Nashville, Tennessee. www.worldpublishing.com. The Old Testament. King Solomon. The Book of Proverbs 3:13-18. Page 291.

as it should be in seminaries. It was taught under the supervision of Bishop Gary Dilly, a well known Roman Catholic exorcist. The first lesson we learned is that we enter into spiritual warfare when we enter into simple prayer. Every time we pray or talk to our Heavenly Father, we end up engaging with our spiritual enemy. We are called to preach and teach and to cast out demons and heal the sick. As we read in chapter six of St. Mark, "and they went out, and preached that men should repent…and they cast our many devils, and anointed with oil many that were sick, and healed them".[100] But when is the last time you heard a preacher talk about casting out demons or exorcising a home or space? It is an understatement to say that an exorcist must have an incredible amount of training, and this is something we should not try on our own without proper supervision. Yet, it is a part of Scripture and it is something of which clergy must have a working knowledge.

As a body of the Christian Church, we have been weakened in our ability and our resolve because of the spiritual lessons of truth and consequences that have been diluted from the pulpit and promulgated by professors and administrators from liberal seminaries over the last half of the twentieth century. This diluted state has left a void in the Church and many Christians today. No longer do we talk about sin, death or consequences since we have been led to believe that there is no hell. We have been led to believe that Satan is no more than a Halloween character. We have been led to believe that a benevolent God could not possibly condemn us to hell. And the fact of the matter is that God does not condemn us because His gift of choice to us has allowed us to condemn ourselves. Many Christians are wandering and seeking answers to our purpose in life. If we read the Scriptures we would realize that we were created to honor, love and serve the Lord our God.

---

[100] Holy Bible, The. (2004). The Holy Bible. *The Holy Bible Authorized King James Version.* World Publishing. Nashville, Tennessee. www.worldpublishing.com. The New Testament. St. Mark. The Gospel according to Mark 6:12-13. Page 441.

Unfortunately, many men and women are looking "for love in all the wrong places"[101] as the song goes.

We are living in a secular humanist world that is consumer driven, market driven and material driven that has developed into a massive rat race or struggle to survive in a "dehumanizing and ultimately futile activity".[102] Quite frankly, many of us are headed into a huge black hole.[103] Our very human natures cannot help but lead us on this highway to nowhere. We are ready for relaxation and need a rest stop. We are yearning for a place where we can clear our minds and spirits from the everyday clutter and find reason to have hope, peace and joy in the substance of sacred theism. Our traditional faith father St. Augustine of Hippo, [104]who was a Roman Catholic Bishop and theologian, wrote in his masterpiece, *The City of God*, that man will be restless until he finds rest in God[105]. This emptiness or void clearly causes the Christian to become unknowing as to who, what, when, where, why and how we believe. Combine that with the distractions offered by an industrial and manufacturing world that provides every means of creature comfort and entertainment, and we find that it leaves no room for a simple and contemplative lifestyle. We bear witness to parents rushing to take their children to every conceivable activity including baseball, football, basketball, softball and soccer practice, dance, music and art lessons to name a few. Elevators, department

---

[101] Lookin' for Love. (1994). Songwriter Waylon Jennings. Country Music Soundtrack. Capitol Records.

[102] Rat Race. (2002). The American Heritage College Dictionary. *The American Heritage College Dictionary Fourth Edition.* Joseph P. Pickett, Vice President and Executive Editor. Published by the Houghton Mifflin Company. Boston Massachusetts. Page 1156.

[103] Black Hole. (2002). The American Heritage College Dictionary. *The American Heritage College Dictionary Fourth Edition.* Joseph P. Pickett, Vice President and Executive Editor. Published by the Houghton Mifflin Company. Boston, Massachusetts. Page 149.

[104] St. Augustine of Hippo. (2005). *Augustine A New Biography.* An Imprint of Harper Collins Publishers. New York, New York. James J. O'Donnell.

[105] City Of God, The. (2006). *The City of God St. Augustine.* Barnes & Noble Library of Essential Reading. Barnes & Noble, Inc. New York, New York. Page 423.

stores and malls are bursting with sounds that keep you captivated and unable to think. Desktops, cell phones, televisions, radios, laptops, and tablets have people wired to them like bees to honey. And we always seem to be in a hurry to go somewhere.

There is a website called LinkedIn[106] where I read a blog under the title 'Anglican Communion'. One of the participants contributed his view of the modern Christian Church. The blog that follows is written by Ifechukwu Ibeme. It is entitled *Metamorphosed Christianity*.

> *"The modern church has metamorphosed to something different from the early church. The thrust in the early church was Moral Purity and Piety; today it is Material Prosperity and Possessions. They sought Grace to fulfill God's requirement; today we seek Favour to obtain our requirements. They sought to be transformed by the Gospel and please God; we seek to transform the Gospel and please ourselves. The early church sought Obedience to God; today the church seeks Abundance from God. The original Devotion and sanctity has now been replaced by the modern goal of Derivation and Success. What shall I render to God has been replaced by what shall I Receive from God? Before, the Giver was the more blessed; today, the Receiver is the more blessed. The old church sought Brokenness before God; today's church seeks Breakthrough from God. Before, Ministrations gripped people with Penitence; today, Ministrations grip people with Excitement. Their holy prophets spoke the Agenda of God; our costly 'prophets' speak the Agenda of man. The old church sought after God for Sacrificial Worship; today's church seeks after God for Beneficial Relationship. The early church*

---

[106] LinkedIn. (2012). Social Media Website for Professionals.

fought to be Different from the world; today's church begs to Conform to the world. The God of the early church was the Judge of all. The 'God' of today's church is judged by all. They would Obey God rather than men; we would Obey men rather than God. Are we still the Church of Christ and His Apostles? IT IS TIME TO SEEK THE LORD".[107]

This blogger supports this view by ending with two Scripture references from Deuteronomy 32:5 which states, "they have corrupted themselves, their spot is not the spot of his children; they are a perverse and crooked generation,"[108] and from Acts 2:40 we read, "and with many other words did he testify and exhort, saying, save yourselves from this untoward (crooked) generation".[109]

We can assume by this blogger's name that he is not from North America which would indicate that the problem with the modern Christian Church is not limited to North America or Europe, but is indeed a worldwide problem. As you can tell there is much truth to his interpretation of today's modern Christian Church. Clearly the Christian Church has metamorphosed and does not appear at all like the ancient Church or the Church of our founding fathers. This blogger offers a clarion call for all Christians to reevaluate our relationship with God in the hope that we return to our roots and find some semblance of the traditional Christian Church. Again,

---

[107] Ifechukwu Ibeme. (2012). Blogger on Professional Social Media Website. LinkedIn. January 20, 2012.

[108] Holy Bible, The. (2004). The Holy Bible. *The Holy Bible Authorized King James Version*. World Publishing. Nashville, Tennessee. www.worldpublishing.com. The Old Testament. The Pentateuch. The Book of Exodus 32:5. Page 104.

[108] Holy Bible, The. (2004). The Holy Bible. The Holy Bible Authorized King James Version. World Publishing. Nashville, Tennessee. www.worldpublishing.com. The Old Testament. The Pentateuch. The Book of Exodus 32:5. Page 104.

[109] Holy Bible, The. (2004). The Holy Bible. *The Holy Bible Authorized King James Version*. World Publishing. Nashville, Tennessee. www.worldpublishing.com. The New Testament. St. Luke. The Acts of the Apostles 2:40. Page 481.

it is very likely that this blogger represents another continent which indicates that our Christian condition is universal. For this reason, it is established with a reasonable certainty that modern Christianity is at a crossroads around the world.

Once again, this is one of the key reasons why this book is written. It offers the basic tools given by the traditional faith of our fathers of Christianity. These tools can help us to find our place in God's creation and the life God has in store for us. When we learn that God created us to be a part of His world to worship Him, to glorify Him, to praise Him, then we have a foundation and threshold to do as Christ told us in the Great Commission to "go ye therefore, and teach all nations, baptizing them in the name of the Father, and of the Son, and of the Holy Ghost; teaching them to observe all things whatsoever I have commanded you: and lo, I am with you always, even unto the end of the world".[110] We learn that God really does love us and to show that infinite love, He gave His only Son Jesus to pay the price for our sins with His blood on that Cross at Calvary. Sin comes with a penalty that can only be paid in blood. For the believers in Christ, our sins were paid in Christ's blood.

I hope this book becomes a companion to the Holy Scriptures and will help you comprehend, discern and understand who we are and how we fit into God's creation. Be mindful that there are times when we have some questions that can never be answered or understood until we reach the next life. At those times we have to rely on our faith. Man's mind is limited while God's mind is unlimited. So often we try to understand God with the limited capacity of our own minds and find that it is impossible to understand His wisdom based on our limited knowledge. As an example, in the *Parable of*

---

[110] Holy Bible, The. (2004). The Holy Bible. *The Holy Bible Authorized King James Version.* World Publishing. Nashville, Tennessee. www.worldpublishing.com. The New Testament. St Matthew. The Gospel of Matthew 28:19-20. Page 437.

the Wedding Feast,[111] found in the Gospel of St. Matthew, Jesus tells us the king invited the good and the not so good to this event. Well, who determined who was good and who was bad? God does not make that determination, man makes that determination. It was man who determined who was good or bad and who then could be invited to the wedding feast. This is an example of man's limited mind and conversely God's unlimited mind. Because our minds are limited, we have the capacity to misunderstand and clearly it is best that God be our judge and not we ourselves because God not only knows what is in our minds but what is in our hearts.

There is no middle ground. One can either be for God or be against God[112]. You cannot be lukewarm[113] or caught in the middle. Your spiritual journey begins by fearing God. Do not be afraid of God, just honor and respect Him as your loving Heavenly Father. God wants you to be a part of His life and for Him to be a part of your life everyday.

---

[111] Holy Bible, The. (2004). The Holy Bible. *The Holy Bible Authorized King James Version.* World Publishing. Nashville, Tennessee. www.worldpublishing.com. The New Testament. St. Matthew. The Gospel of Matthew 22:2-14. Pages 432-433.

[112] ESV Study Bible.(2008). *English Study Bible English Standard Version.* Crossway Bibles. A publishing ministry of Good News Publishers. Wheaton, Illinois. St. Mark. The Gospel of Mark 9: 40. Page 1913.

[113] Holy Bible, The. (2004). The Holy Bible. The Holy Bible Authorized King James Version. World Publishing. Nashville, Tennessee. www.worldpublishing.com. The New Testament. St. John. The Book of Revelation 3:16. Page 545.

Chapter Eight

In Unity and Godly Love

"The Lord by wisdom hath founded the earth; by understanding hath he established the heavens. By His knowledge the depths are broken up, and the clouds drop down the dew".[114]

It is not difficult to see the results of secular humanism on our national institutions. Had we remained faithful to the practices of sacred theism we would not be in the near tragic state of affairs we find ourselves in today. The divided body of the Christian Church is an example of the seeds of discontent that have been harvested with its dozens of mainstream denominations and hundreds if not thousands of independent assemblies. It has disheartened and disappointed me for some time. It is not the Christian doctrine that has unsettled me; it the behavior of the church members who disappoint me. In fact, it kept me from attending seminary for many years and then serving in the ministry that God had planned for me. I had to learn that the Church is a haven for sinners and that means they bring their issues with them to Church and sometimes those issues are brought out in the open. Ultimately, the transgressions of sinners in the Church did not succeed in keeping me out of the ministry for God had a plan and purpose in store for

---

[114] Holy Bible, The. (2004). The Holy Bible. *The Holy Bible Authorized King James Version*. World Publishing. Nashville, Tennessee. www.worldpublishing.com. The Old Testament. King Solomon. The Book of Proverbs 3:19-20. Page 291.

me. I know that I am a sinner too and I need the church as much as anyone to help restore and cleanse me in my daily walks with God.

In my earliest recollections of church life, Church members seemed to be primarily focused on incidentals and behavior instead of true doctrine. It seemed that those who raised their voices the loudest were the ones who had the least amount of theological training, Scripture knowledge or prayer life. However, in most cases we defend our personal incidental peculiarities and behavior and claim it to be theological doctrine. Add the fact that many Christians believe they have a right to interpret the Holy Scriptures on their own rather than trust and rely on trained and educated clergy. This combination gives us a cornucopia of ideas pushing to change doctrine to meet many naive views of Scripture. If we apply ourselves to the study of Scripture and when it is interpreted correctly, then we realize it should be looked at as the whole and not viewed in bits and pieces.

Did you know that there are some verses of Scripture that are not intended for everyone to understand? In St. Luke we read, "Then the disciples asked Him, saying, 'What does this parable mean'? And He said, 'To you it has been given to know the mysteries of the kingdom of God, but to the rest it is given in parables, that 'seeing they may not see, and hearing they may not understand.'"[115] And again in the Gospel of Luke we read, "but they understood none of these things: this saying was hidden from them, and they did not know the things which were spoken".[116] Consequently, here is the scenario we find ourselves in today. We have people who have no theological training who claim they understand and know the meaning of the Word of God, and yet two thousand years ago, the very disciples who lived and ate and talked to Jesus Christ in His presence, said they did not know what Jesus' parables meant. Now

---

[115] Believer's Study Bible, The. (1991). The Believer's Study Bible. *The Believer's Study Bible New King James Version.* Thomas Nelson Publishers. Nashville, Tennessee. The New Testament. St. Luke. The Gospel of Luke 8:9-10. Page 1452.

[116] Believer's Study Bible, The. (1991).The Believer's Study Bible. *The Believer's Study Bible New King James Version.* Thomas Nelson Publishers. Nashville, Tennessee. The New Testament. St. Luke. The Gospel of Luke 18:34. Page 1474.

you must decide who you want to believe. In Jesus' day, He would take His disciples away from the crowds and explain the parable's meaning. Today, we have clergy who meet this need and know how to properly interpret Scripture. Where many are at fault is that they look at the Scripture on face value and do not dig deeper to find the whole truth.

Many of these self-proclaimed interpreters of Scripture often look with a level of disdain for those who were seminary trained. Still others become self-ordained or have been ordained by their earthly father or a group of well-meaning men. Then there are others who claim that God spoke to them personally or that they are enlightened by the Holy Ghost. Many cult leaders fall into this category. David Koresh, of the Branch Davidian comes to mind as an example of a self-proclaimed representative of God who caused the deaths of many of his followers in Waco, Texas in 1993. Then there was Jim Jones of San Francisco's People's Temple who eventually poisoned hundreds of his followers in the jungles of Guiana, South America. They think they may be listening to God, but in many cases it is their own minds they are hearing or perhaps the devil himself to whom they are talking because they report what they want to hear, not what God wants them to hear. Often they pick one specific verse and build their entire theology or doctrine around that verse.

On the other hand, there are many who are not of a cult but are devout Christians and are well-intentioned with hearts of gold but they are often fundamental and are void of in-depth training. This point is underscored when a few weeks ago I was in Books-a-Million book store perusing the aisles when I stumbled upon a book entitled *Learn the Bible in 24 Hours*. Well, more power to them if they think they can learn four thousand years of theological history in twenty-four hours. It has taken me over fifty years of study and the more I study, the more I realize how much more there is to learn. Fundamentals are important as a starting point but one must build on them. Unfortunately, this is how many Christians want their relationship with God. They want it now like a fast food restaurant with little or no effort or they want it from the effort of someone else. They are lacking the discipline for daily devotion and Bible study and the fellowship of worship services that over years gives us the wisdom we seek.

I know that many denominations sprang forth from the Protestant Reformation roughly five hundred years ago and many more did so especially in the last two hundred years. Many have based their entire doctrines on one of the following such as the Great Commission, Speaking in Tongues, Washing of Feet, the Seventy, the One Hundred Forty-Four Thousand, and Predestination to name a few. Some even serve Kool-Aid[117] instead of wine for Holy Eucharist which only implies that they fail to comprehend the majesty and omnipotence of God. Why would anyone want to discredit the magnificence of God by serving flavored water? Then there are others who charm poisonous snakes as their way of worshiping God. When we deny God's power or rest our entire doctrine on one verse in order to entertain the masses, then we are ultimately selling snake oil and are leading astray those who are searching for the true gospel of Christ.

There appears to be a short-sightedness on the part of denominations that were established in the last two hundred years versus the traditional denominations such as the Eastern Orthodox, Anglican Catholic and Roman Catholic who trace their unbroken foundations back to the Protestant Reformation and even to the days of Jesus Christ and the Apostles. In many cases they take one point of Scripture and use it as their unique foundation of church doctrine and go about building a following based on that premise. This is a naive view of Scripture. I do not wish to simplify this premise because my point is to show how we fail to interpret correctly the whole of Scripture. Suffice it to say that as an example of this shortsightedness, there is a denomination that bases its doctrine largely on speaking in tongues. No doubt, speaking in tongues is one of the gifts of the Spirit. In I Corinthians, we read, *"Do all have the gifts of healings? Do all speak with tongues? Do all interpret? But earnestly desire the best gifts. And yet I show you*

---

[117] Kool- Aid. (1927). A water based flavored concentrate drink invented by Edwin Perkins. Hastings, Nebraska. Kraft Food Company.

a more excellent way".[118] (The greatest gift is love.) Followers of this denomination believe that if they do not speak in tongues[119], then they are not saved. But in I Corinthians chapter fourteen we read, *"He who speaks in a tongue edifies himself, but he who prophesies edifies the church. I wish you all spoke with tongues, but even more that you prophesied; for he who prophesies is greater than he who speaks with tongues, unless indeed he interprets, that the church may receive edification"*.[120] Here in this verse, even the Apostle Paul admits that not everyone who is saved can speak in tongues. Further, you will be hard pressed to attend a service where an interpreter is present. I have been to more than one of these services and never heard anyone interpret. The Scripture says you are not allowed to speak in tongues unless someone is there to interpret. It is my understanding that only God can read the heart of a man and He is the judge. In fact, He tells us *"judge not, that ye be not judged"*.[121] Therefore, I hope I do not appear to be judgmental of other denominations whose method of worship is not traditional. I do believe they are sincere, but fail to understand the historical need for the traditional faith of our fathers.

Then, if we look in chapter sixteen of the Gospel of Mark, we read, *"and these signs will follow who believe: In my name they will cast out demons; they will speak with new tongues; they will take up serpents; and if they drink anything deadly, it will by no means*

---

[118] Believer's Study Bible, The. (1991). The Believer's Study Bible. *The Believer's Study Bible New King James Version*. Thomas Nelson Publishers. Nashville, Tennessee. The New Testament. St. Paul. The first Letter of Paul to the Corinthians 12:30-31. Page 1638.

[119] Believer's Study Bible, The. (1991). The Believer's Study Bible. *The Believer's Study Bible New King James Version*. Thomas Nelson Publishers. Nashville, Tennessee. The New Testament. St. Paul. The first Letter of Paul to the Corinthians 12:1-31. Pages 1635-1640.

[120] Believer's Study Bible, The. (1991). The Believer's Study Bible. *The Believer's Study Bible New King James Version*. Thomas Nelson Publishers. Nashville Tennessee. The New Testament. St. Paul. The first Letter of Paul to the Corinthians 14:4-5. Pages 1639-1640.

[121] Holy Bible, The. (2004). The Holy Bible. *The Holy Bible Authorized King James Version*. World Publishing. Nashville, Tennessee. www.worldpublishing.com. The Old Testament. St. Matthew. The Gospel of Matthew 7:1. Page 423.

hurt them; they will lay hands on the sick, and they will recover".[122] This is a good example of splintered sects or denominations that interpret the Scripture on face value and do not comprehend the entirety of the whole gospel. This verse addresses two groups; one that speaks in tongues and the other that handles serpents. Those believers who belong to these denominations are, I believe, sincere and genuine. However, they are largely misguided. I have chosen briefly to address the speaking in tongues issue as an example because volumes of books have been written on the subject. And as far as handling serpents or drinking anything deadly, I believe those who do so are missing the point. Allow me to address this issue by using another of Jesus' parables. Jesus talks in the Gospel of Matthew about looking at a woman lustfully, and if he did he would already have committed adultery in his heart.[123] He further instructs that one who did this should gouge out his eye and throw it away as it is better to lose a part of your body than your whole body to be thrown in hell. Jesus adds, *"If your right hand sins cut it off and throw it away for it is better to lose a hand than to lose your whole body and go to hell".* Do we think these graphic images are what Christ really meant for us to do? I think not. If our eye wanders, we should repent and look the other way. We are not to desecrate or malign our bodies. Our hands are of no use to the needy if we sever them. Allow our appendages to give a helping hand to others rather than ending our service to God by maiming ourselves. This is an example of understanding the whole of Scripture and not aligning ourselves to one unique verse. By being emphatic in His description, Christ was able to make His point and no one failed to understand Him.

---

[122] Believer's Study Bible, The. (1991). The Believer's Study Bible. *The Believer's Study Bible New King James Version.* Thomas Nelson Publishers. Nashville, Tennessee. The New Testament. St. Mark. The Gospel of Mark 16:17-18. Page 1428.

[123] Believer's Study Bible, The. (1991). The Believer's Study Bible. *The Believer's Study Bible New King James Version.* Thomas Nelson Publishers. Nashville, Tennessee. The New Testament. St. Matthew. The Gospel of Matthew 5:27-30. Page 1343.

Another example was when I found myself in front of a fundamentalist preacher who was peppering me with theological questions and then asked if my denomination washed feet. I replied that we do but not on a regular basis. His conclusion and response was that we must be OK then. I thought to myself, "What do you mean OK? Are you implying that if we did not wash each other's feet, then we are not OK and therefore must not be a Christian?" Here is another example of taking selected verses of Scripture and creating doctrine or dogma to meet the closed interpretation. Those that incorporate these practices are more like the Pharisees who were the protectors of the law but were completely lost in the understanding of what the Scriptures teach and what Christ meant when he gave us the Gospel. This strengthens the argument that clergy should have a seminary background. Debates on these issues facing the church's doctrines are regularly debated in seminary classes where sound learning is taught and false doctrine does not creep into the minds of people who interpret them. I might add that it is largely from those who are not properly schooled that false doctrines have been planted and the seeds of apostasy have developed as exemplified by David Koresh and others.

As we know and understand Church history, we need to acknowledge that from the beginning of Christ's establishment of Christianity, we were all catholic or universal which is what catholic means. In terms of unity and Godly love, we need to be concerned about the development of Christian doctrine and practices. A new way of worship is not always best. Perhaps there is a need for better communication so we can better understand how God wants us to worship Him.

We should be aware of and alert to any creeping doctrine or dogma that is not consistent with God's Word. We need to take ownership of ourselves and our relationship with God. Let no one believe that our minister will stand in judgment of our sins. We have the ultimate responsibility for how we behave and how we act. We cannot point our fingers at others for our shortcomings and sin. Properly trained clergy are good sources of knowledge if they preach and teach the Word of God. As I wrote earlier, our seminaries are not what they used to be but they are still better than following the lead of untrained clergy. No doubt, the seeds of secular humanism have infiltrated the hallowed halls of seminaries as they have every other institution of our society. But there are sincere students there who continue to abide by the principles of sacred theism and if we find them we will be the better for it. Also, if you find yourself in a church that is preaching and teaching a doctrine of psychology or sociology and not theology, then you need to find yourself another church in which to worship.

Ultimately, we as Christians have to *"trust in the Lord with all thine heart and lean not to thine own understanding"*.[124] We will do ourselves a service if we take to heart the *Summary of the Law* which Christ gave to us in the New Testament. The *Summary of the Law* will be discussed in detail in the first segment of Part Two, so I will end this short story here and I will expound on the *summary* in that later segment.

---

[124] Holy Bible, The. (2004). The Holy Bible. *The Holy Bible Authorized King James Version.* World Publishing. Nashville, Tennessee. www.worldpublishing.com. The Old Testament. King Solomon. The Book of Proverbs 3:5. Page 291.

Chapter Nine

The Prodigal Son

"My son, let not them depart from thine eyes; keep sound wisdom and discretion; So shall they be life unto thy soul, and grace to thy neck. Then shalt thou walk in thy way safely, and thy foot shall not stumble. When thou liest down, thou shalt not be afraid; yea, thou shalt lie down, and thy sleep shall be sweet".[125]

I tried to walk the tightrope of traditional moral behavior and maintain a life based on the principles of sacred theism. For this reason, I have included my personal experience in this book because it covers the recent historical development in tandem and gives the reader a personal view of the battles that many wage in this war of good versus evil.

In my spiritual journey, I grew up in a loving Christian home. It would be misleading if I were to claim it was perfect in every way but it probably was as perfect as perfect can be. This definition of perfection is based on the criteria that only Christ was perfect. I have wonderful Christian parents, Paul and Lorene, and two Christian brothers; Ronnie, my identical twin, and Michael, the first-born. We have another brother Stephen who was taken to be

---

[125] Holy Bible, The. (2004). The Holy Bible. *The Holy Bible Authorized King James Version.* World Publishing. Nashville, Tennessee. www.worldpublishing.com. The Old Testament. King Solomon. The Book of Proverbs. 3:21-24. Page 291.

in the Lord's care in 1954 when he was just three days old. My parents practiced good parenting skills and abilities and we were all well fed, housed, protected and nurtured. These skills they learned from their parents and grandparents. We lived in a modest brick home in a nice neighborhood. We were given every opportunity to excel in education and sports. My parents made sure we went to church when the doors were open and we conformed to the doctrine of St. Paul who in his Letter to the Ephesians said,"… do not provoke your children to anger, but bring them up in the discipline and instruction of the Lord".[126]

Our childhood was in every way like the hit television series at the time, "The Andy Griffith Show" [127]featuring the town of Mayberry with the loving characters of Opie, Andy, Barney, Gomer, and Aunt Bee not to mention the many other wholesome family characters. This show originated in the sixties and has been in syndication reruns ever since. It joins the genre of family viewing such as the Dick Van Dyke Show[128] or the I Love Lucy Show,[129] or The Red Skelton Comedy Hour[130], when standards of behavior meant something. This was a time when you could watch television and not be concerned with what your children would hear or be exposed to. These shows were family-oriented and they often delivered a moral lesson. Sadly, this is not the case today.

---

[126] ESV Study Bible. (2008). *ESV Study Bible English Standard Version.* Crossway Bibles. A publishing ministry of Good News Publishers. Wheaton, Illinois. The New Testament. St. Paul. Letter to the Ephesians 6:4. Page 2272.

[127] Andy Griffith Show, The. (1960-1968). *The Andy Griffith Show.* Produced by Aaron Rueben and Bob Ross. Desilu Studios. Culver City, California. Columbia Broadcasting System Network. www.tvland.com.

[128] Dick Van Dyke Show, The. (1961-1966). *The Dick Van Dyke Show.* Executive Producer Sheldon Leonard. Producers Carl Reiner, Bill Persky, Sam Denoff. Columbia Broadcasting System Network. www.tvland.com.

[129] I Love Lucy Show, The. (1962-1968). *The I Love Lucy Show.* Produced by Dezi Arnaz and Elliott Lewis. Desilu Studios. Culver City, California. Columbia Broadcasting System Network. www.tvland.com

[130] Red Skelton Hour, The. (1951-1971). *The Red Skelton Hour.* Produced by Guy Della-Cioppa. Desilu Productions. CBS Television City, Hollywood, California. National Broadcasting System and Columbia Broadcasting System Networks. www.tvland.com.

Today, it is difficult to watch the sitcoms on television for the unlimited references to sex and the cursing, as well as the visual innuendo in reference to immorality. Even commercials are sometimes difficult to watch for their allusion to immoral behavior. Not only is there profanity, but far too often there are the degrading curse words and blasphemy directed against our Heavenly Father. The traditional family of one man and one woman in marriage is ridiculed, while unwed mothers and homosexual lifestyles are heralded as the noble way of life to be mimicked and approved. Media standards are not what they used to be for it is clear that anything goes and there appear to be no standards of decent public behavior. The only prescription we have left to protect ourselves from indecent behavior, foul language or sexual innuendo on television is the remote control. It is nominally effective in censoring images and sounds of bad behavior.

The new seeds of change and secular humanism took hold in the sixties and seventies although they were planted centuries earlier. I do believe the assassinations of the thirty-fifth United States President John F. Kennedy[131] in 1963, and his brother United States Senator Robert Kennedy,[132] as well as Civil Rights Leader the Rev. Martin Luther King[133] had a profound and lingering effect on the psyche of America. The Vietnam War also had an impact on all levels of society, especially the youth of this country, and made fertile ground for the seeds of secular humanism to take hold, grow, and mature. The youth were bewildered and were looking for something to hold on to that seemed real, not surreal. The presence of television in every household as well as market-driven advertising led to the proliferation and glorification of materialism.

---

[131] President John F. Kennedy. (2001). Random House College Dictionary. *Random House Webster's College Dictionary 2nd Revised and Updated Edition*. Random House, Inc. New York, New York. www.randomhouse.com. Page 726.

[132] Senator Robert F. Kennedy. (2001) Random House College Dictionary. *Random House College Webster's Dictionary 2nd Revised and Updated Edition*. Random House, Inc. New York, New York. www.randomhouse.com. Page 726.

[133] Reverend Martin Luther King. (1997). Microsoft Encarta 97 Encyclopedia. *Microsoft Encarta 97 Encyclopedia*. Redmond, Washington. Microsoft Encarta 1997 Encyclopedia.

It appears everyone bought into this marketing bonanza. For many, secular humanism with its materialistic warehouses gave them something tangible on which to rely.

I grew up in the South, sometimes known as the "Bible Belt".[134] This region of the United States has held this distinction for decades and it is based on the large majority of mostly protestant evangelical Christians living in this region of the country. These Christians have a fundamental view of life through the Holy Scriptures and believe in the inherent freedoms of religion, speech, right of assembly, and the right to bear arms which they feel are sacred to our United States Constitution[135].

My hometown of Florence, South Carolina was just another sleepy southern country town nestled in the tobacco, corn, soybean, and cotton fields of the Great Pee Dee River Basin until the last few years. It is now a college town and regional commercial hub for the Pee Dee region of the state. My childhood was filled with fishing and hunting trips, skinny dipping in local ponds, and walking through the Southern pine woods chasing rabbits, squirrels and birds with our faithful friend, our beagle named Limbo. Here, in the South, it was important who your family was, not where your father worked. Everyone attended church on Sunday and went to Wednesday night prayer service every week. Family reunions were an annual event that kept the family tied to one another over shared values, beliefs, and time.

Unfortunately, when I entered my twenties, the magnetism of the bright lights of this world caused me to depart from my parental religious instruction for the better part of a decade. On the heels of my graduation from college and upon returning from an eighteen week pilgrimage to Western Europe and the Scandinavian countries, I began a life experiencing the virtues or vices of this

---

[134] Bible Belt. (2001). Random House College Dictionary. *Random House Webster's College Dictionary 2nd Revised and Updated Edition.* Random House, Inc. New York, New York. www.randomhouse.com. Page 130.

[135] United States Constitution. (1997). Microsoft Encarta 97 Encyclopedia. *Microsoft Encarta 97 Encyclopedia.* Redmond, Washington. Microsoft Encarta 97 Encyclopedia.

world. I look back on one fateful day as a turning point, for I made a conscious and specific decision in my early twenties that I now consider with regret, for it was on that day that I turned my back on God. It would be irresponsible for me to point to anyone or anything that caused me to make that decision. I suppose I lived a sheltered life through high school, and the impact of a liberal arts culture and the diversity of public opinion where people's morals and behavior are on different levels, caused me to take a second look and examine my threshold of beliefs and values. No doubt, the social, political, legal, medical, and religious areas of our society had a combined effect on me as my resistance to sin began to unravel. And, no doubt the secular humanism was wearing away my armor of sacred theism that I had developed during my childhood.

However, God's plan for me was restored and it finally took hold of me after about a decade or more experiencing a prodigal son's life. God brought me back home to my core values and beliefs that are steeped in sacred theism. I am eternally grateful that He saved me physically, emotionally, and spiritually from this decade of debauchery as I know of many who did not survive this wayward lifestyle. It now seems, looking back, that I had to reach rock bottom and that came at the end of a divorce when I lost custody of my daughter and I found myself in a downward state of despair.

Then, I met a wonderful Christian woman who became my wife. She is the granddaughter of a Southern Methodist minister. Her life's story was not much different from mine, although it is her story to tell, so we felt that God brought us together to build a safe haven in our home to share our love for family and our love for the worship of our Heavenly Father and His Son. We refer to our safe haven as our sanctuary for it is here that we find peace, rest and joy from an outside world that is all but peaceful, joyous or restful. In our sanctuary we feel that God protects us from a harmful and destructive world. We rely on the verse in Exodus wherein the Lord replied, "*my presence is with you, and I will give you rest,"*[136] as well as the verse in Joshua, *"as for me and my house, we will serve the Lord"*.[137]

The Holy Scriptures warn us of a Satan who is roaming the earth like a roaring lion and he is out to devour us. If you have never visited a zoo and heard a roaring lion, then you should take the time for as the sound of a roaring lion will surely send shivers up your spine and make the hair stand-up on the back of your neck. Always be aware that when you are in the face of danger, the power of the Holy Spirit who dwells in you is there to protect you if you call on Him. This underscores the message for Christians that the power within us is greater than the power that is in the world.

In the New Testament book of I John we read, *"For whatever is born of God overcomes the world. And this is the victory that has overcome the world—our faith. Who is he who overcomes the world, but he who believes that Jesus is the Son of God"*?[138] Thus, in I Peter we read that we are to, *"be sober, be vigilant: because your adversary the devil walks about like a roaring lion, seeking whom he may devour. Resist him, steadfast in the faith, knowing that the same sufferings are experienced by your brotherhood in the world. But may the God of all grace, who called us to His eternal glory by Christ Jesus, after you have suffered a while, perfect, establish, strengthen and settle you"*.[139] As you can see, I have quoted several

---

[136] Seasons of Reflection. (1996). *Seasons of Reflection New International Version Bible in 365 Daily Readings with Special Helps on Prayer.* The International Bible Society. Colorado Springs, Colorado. The Old Testament. The Pentateuch. Moses. The Book of Exodus 33:14. Page 170.

[137] Seasons of Reflection. (1996). *Seasons of Reflection New International Version Bible in 365 Daily Readings with Special Helps on Prayer.* The International Bible Society. Colorado Springs, Colorado. The Old Testament. The Book of Joshua 24:15. Page 378.

[138] Orthodox Study Bible, The. (2008). The Orthodox Study Bible. *The Orthodox Study Bible New King James Version.* St. Athanasius Academy Septuagint. Thomas Nelson Publishers. Thomas Nelson, Inc. Nashville, Tennessee. The New Testament. St. John. The first Book of John 5:4-5. Page 1703.

[139] Orthodox Study Bible, The. (2008). The Orthodox Study Bible. *The Orthodox Study Bible New King James Version.* St. Athanasius Academy Septuagint. Thomas Nelson Publishers. Thomas Nelson, Inc. Nashville, Tennessee. The Old Testament. St. Peter. The first Book of Peter 5:7-9. Page 1689.

Scripture verses in this article. I quote them because they gave me the wisdom, hope, and strength I needed to help me navigate the troubled waters I was sailing in during my prodigal years. I have included these verses of Holy Scripture in this chapter because they gave me hope and comfort in those dark and, at times, dreary days. And if you find yourself in a similar situation, I hope they will give you the same hope and comfort they gave me. Do not despair, for help is on the way, and it is in the name and person of Jesus Christ. He will save you now and eternally if only you let him and repent, turn away from your wayward life and ask Him to be your Lord and Savior.

One day, I pray you will find a sanctuary as we have where we are nurtured through the Holy Spirit in a revelation of hope, peace, and joy. Outside of our home we face an ominous world which, although illuminated by the sun, is full of defeat and despair. We enter the world to bring forth the light that shines from Jesus Christ who is in us and is the light of the world. He shines through us and we are His beacon or lighthouse to a lost and lonely world. Our lives can and have been restored by God's grace and mercy. Our two beautiful daughters Tiffany and Cathleen have given us five wonderful grandchildren. We are blessed with three grandsons; Joshua, Tyler and Andrew; and two granddaughters, Grace and Savannah. The crucible of life's fire and brimstone has tempered me by all my family relationships and through it all God has molded me into the person I am today. Cynthia, my wife, and I have weathered good times and bad times but our love for each other is unyielding and unwavering. Our life's trials and tribulations have strengthened our relationship with God and each other. God continues to mold us in our lives to make us stronger and more resilient every day. It does not necessarily make life any easier, because a Christian's life is not an easy road to travel, but as our wisdom accrues, we will find that our decisions will not cause us to stumble as often. As we draw closer to God, then we grow closer to each other. When we take our eyes and thoughts away from God, then we begin to drift in the wrong direction. However, if we remain disciplined and focused, then thankfully we will waver less often. When we do drift away, God has a way of reeling us in again. And if you read the *Parable of the Lost Son*[140] in Luke you will see that I share the same enthusiasm that the prodigal son experienced when in my thirties I became reconciled with God. Like the prodigal son, I have returned from my wayward ways and I have been restored into the comforting and protecting arms of my Heavenly Father. Therefore, my greatest delight in being close to my Heavenly Father is the inescapable peace and joy that He grants me.

There are many prodigal sons and daughters in our world. Many believe they are a lost cause because of their lifestyle choices and their wayward ways and many addictions. They do not believe that they have the will power, discipline or ability to end their bad habits or change their self-centered lives. I know how difficult it can be as I have been there. I lived with addictions for many years and it took a major effort to turn things around. I bear witness that anyone can overcome any addiction or wayward lifestyle with God's help and a commitment to change for the better. You owe it to yourself at least to try. You only have one life to give. God can restore you to a life of hope, peace, and joy if only you let him. God is waiting on you and wants you in his protective arms. The world of secular humanism does not have to keep you in its grip and enslave you. Choose a life of sacred theism and you will not look back or regret having done so. You will reap a better, healthier, and more joyous life for making that choice of life over death and good over evil.

---

[140] Apologetics Study Bible, The. (2007). The Apologetics Study Bible. *Understand Why You Believe The Apologetics Study Bible New English Standard Version.* Holman Christian Standard Bible. Holman Bible Publishers. Nashville, Tennessee. The New Testament. St. Luke. The Gospel of Luke 15:11-32. Pages 1545-1546.

Chapter Ten

The Spiritual Journey

"Be not afraid of sudden fear, neither of the desolation of the wicked, when it cometh. For the Lord shall be thy confidence, and shall keep thy foot from being taken".[141]

Individually, I will liken my walk to Brother Lawrence, [142]a seventeenth century European monk who maintained a constant conversation with God. He recorded many of his thoughts and discussions with God in his diary which we have the benefit of reading today. When we compare his writings to ourselves, we are given insight not only to who we are as created man and woman, but who we are in our relationship with God. As a personal practice, I often do not say, "amen", when I complete my prayers to God. To me this is like hanging up the telephone receiver or ending a conversation on my cellular telephone. I practice this because I desire to remain in constant connection with my Heavenly Father and the only way I can see to avoid saying goodbye is not to "hang up the telephone". Brother Lawrence is probably one of our best

---

[141] Holy Bible, The. (2004). The Holy Bible. *The Holy Bible Authorized Version.* World Publishing. Nashville, Tennessee. www.worldpublishing.com. The Old Testament. King Solomon. The Book of Proverbs 3:25-26. Page 291.

[142] Brother Lawrence. (2009). *The Practice of the Presence of God: Being Conversations and Letters of Nicholas Herman of Lorraine, Brother Lawrence.* Christian Books Today, Ltd. Chorley, Lancashire, United Kingdom. www.christianbookstoday.com.

examples of one who lived a sacred theistic life not because he lived a monastic life, but because he kept God at the center of his life. It is very appropriate that I include a short story that includes Brother Lawrence as a key character.

Not too many years ago, I completed my second unit of Clinical Pastoral Education at Moore Regional Hospital in Pinehurst, North Carolina. This specialized training included four hundred hours of intensive psychotherapy training. Together with my first unit of CPE, I now possess a total of eight hundred hours of clinical psychotherapy training. This program is led by the able psychologist, Dr. Beverly Jessup, D. Min. Dr. Jessup is also an ordained minister in the Brotherhood (Quakers) and the son of a Southern Methodist minister. It was in one of Dr. Jessup's classes that I heard or read from one of the many textbooks, or perhaps from a conversation I had with a classmate, that when God created Adam, he was "wired" for God. What that means is that God created us to stay in constant communication with Him. It is like an electrical plug connected to a receptacle. As long as the plug is connected, then there is a constant source of electrical energy that travels through and emanates from it. However, if the plug is disconnected from the receptacle then there is no longer a connection and thereby is no longer a source of energy or power. If you unplug an electrical device then it will cease to work. The same scenario works with us. If we are our only source of power or energy, then we have a very limited source of power. However, if we decide to "power up" and connect to God, then we have an unlimited source of energy, and our strength and power is immeasurable. As for those energy drinks on the market today, you may want to save your money and get your energy from God.

We need to be wired to God, as only with Him can we practice the tenets of sacred theism and defend ourselves from the powers of secular humanism. In my spiritual journey, I have experienced moments of inspiration. Often that inspiration comes to me when I am taking a hot shower. I do not know if it is the symbolism of the water that is covering me that seems to be cleansing me of my sins so that I am in a state of purity in the sight of God, or that I am naked and vulnerable and in a state that I am most receptive to His words in my heart and in my soul. In either case, I welcome His inspiration for me daily. These times of inspiration are not limited to hot showers. Sometimes God reveals Himself to me when I am driving down the highway or interstate in the silence of my vehicle cabin when the radio is off. This corridor is symbolic of the highway of life or an artery that directs the life giving blood to the parts of our body that renew, strengthen and nourish us. Sometimes God speaks to me in my dreams as we read in Acts 2:17, *"And it shall come to pass in the last days, says God, that I will pour out My Spirit on all flesh: Your sons and your daughters shall prophesy, your young men shall see visions, Your old men shall dream dreams"*. As you can see I include myself in the last category.

I learned the value of silence from the monks at Mepkin Abby. One of the best ways to hear God is when we are silent and listening. If there is noise or we are talking with one another, we cannot possibly hear God when He wants to talk to us. We have to develop the inner ear or spiritual ear where God talks. Silence is a valuable commodity and something we should cherish as it also gives us peace and rests our spirits. God also talks to me in my dreams. There are many examples of God speaking to people in their dreams recorded in the Holy Scriptures. But dreams are not the only way God speaks to us. He speaks to us through His creation. He may speak to us through songs and hymns and music. God is not limited in ways He chooses to communicate with us.

There are many lessons to be learned from a spiritual journey. Some people take sabbaticals for extended weeks or months at a time. Everyone's spiritual journey is unique. My months in Europe in the seventies are counted as part of a lifelong spiritual journey. I had the chance to participate in a focus group observing Dr. Frances Schafer who is a well known 20th century theologian. His life's work was compiled in a book and documentary called *How Should We Then Live*. It was one of the highlights of my journey to travel and live in the Alps of central Europe in the country of Switzerland. God revealed Himself to me in the beautiful peaks and valleys of that beautiful country.

Spiritual journeys can occur over a period of days or weeks. My days living at Mepkin Abby left a lasting impression on me. From the memory of those days I came to understand the need for silence and meditation in the development of my relationship with God. It has strengthened me as I apply the precepts and concepts of a sacred theistic life. I recommend that everyone take a spiritual journey at some point in their life and make it a lifetime experience.

Finally, I would like to include one last comment on being wired to God. In the 14th chapter of the Gospel of John beginning at the 15th verse we read, *"If you love me, you will obey what I command. And I will ask the Father, and He will give you another Counselor, to be with you forever--the Spirit of Truth. The world cannot accept him nor knows him. But you know him, for he lives with you and will be in you. I will not leave you orphans; I will come to you. Before long, the world will not see me anymore, but you will see me. Because I live, you also live. On that day you will realize that I am in my Father, and you are in me, and I am in you. Whoever has my commands and obeys them, he is the one who loves me. He who loves me will be loved by My Father, and I too will love him and show myself to him"*. This verse from the New Testament shows us that we are wired to God if we believe in Him and accept Jesus as our Lord and Savior and live by His commandments. You are not alone in this world so you do not have to be lonely. God is with us every step of our life's journey. Meditate in silence and let Him speak to you and you will live a joyful and rewarding life. When you find that place, share it with others so that the light that brightens you will help brighten up an otherwise dark world.

Chapter Eleven

The Disunity Continues

"Withhold not good from them to whom it is due, when it is in the power of thine hand to do it. Say not unto thy neighbor, Go, and come again, and tomorrow I will give: when thou hast it by thee, devise not evil against thy neighbor, seeing he dwelleth securely by thee. Strive not with a man without cause, if he hath done thee no harm. Envy thou not the oppressor, and choose none of his ways. For the froward is abomination to the Lord: but his secret is with the righteous".[143]

Now that I have shared some of my theological background and development as an example of the perils and the impact of secular humanism on me and ultimately on our society, and how it seems to overwhelm sacred theism, let us turn to the subject of the "cultural war" I mentioned in the first short story entitled *The Scope of the Battlefield.*

Historically, the Christian Church is the catholic church. Catholic means universal and in the Anglican Book of Common Prayer believers acknowledge the One Holy Catholic and Apostolic Church. The first break or schism in the church occurred around

---

[143] Holy Bible, The. (2004). The Holy Bible. *The Holy Bible Authorized King James Version.* World Publishing. Nashville, Tennessee. www.worldpublishing.com. The Old Testament. King Solomon. The Book of Proverbs 3:27-32. Page 291.

1000 A.D. when the Western Church seated in Rome and the Eastern Church seated in Constantinople (which is now Istanbul, Turkey) decided to go their separate ways. Around five hundred years later, the Western Church split again in a schism that was called the Protestant Reformation. I sometimes liken the word Protestant Reformation to 'Protesters Revolution.'

This protest was largely attributed to Martin Luther who had legitimate issues with the Roman Catholic Church as well as his earthly father. His difficult relationship with his earthly father translated into a difficult relationship with his Heavenly Father according to many psychotherapists and researchers and much has been written on the subject. I am not suggesting the strain of the relationship with his earthly father who wanted him to become a barrister rather than a member of the clergy, diminished the sobering wrongs he highlighted in his Ninety-Five Theses; or that he was not responsible of his actions. Rather, I am suggesting what many astute scholars have said before of what could be the source of his motivations. He highlighted the wrongful practices of the Roman clergy which regularly included the selling of indulgences for personal gain, the practice of nepotism in church offices, the wrongful practice of priests marrying outside the sacrament, and the fathering of children outside of wedlock. Indeed these were serious errors by the Roman Catholic clergy and they needed to be corrected with punishments to fit the crimes. There may not have been civil laws broken, but surely there were canon (church) laws which were broken. All these abuses violated the canons of the Roman Catholic Church and made liars, thieves and adulterers of the guilty clergy. This did not give priests an honorable reputation. Certainly these errant priests or anyone associated with them, or anyone behaving like them, are not who God wants representing Him, then or now.

Like many revolutions, the Protestant Reformation went well beyond what was necessary to correct the crimes, circumstances or abuses that caused the split. In the process it totally changed the shape of the church and the society it represented. The Bolshevik Revolution in Russia in the early twentieth century comes to mind as a revolution that went well beyond the necessity for correction of errors. In Russia's case they became a Communist state which was a dramatic change from a Monarchy. It was like a pendulum swinging from one extreme to another. In Rome's case, the Church split between those who would remain Roman Catholic and those who became Protestant. Wars have always changed the landscape of the world and the Protestant Reformation can be viewed as no less than a war for the souls of men.

Some of the areas where the Protestant Reformation went too far were in areas such as the ending of ritual and tradition in church services. We bear witness to this change in many of the Protestant churches today. Additionally, most of the Protestant denominations broke with the Apostolic Succession with the one exception of the Anglican Church. In other words, the "revolutionaries" went too far in their responses to the initial grievances and developed a new approach to worship altogether. This is more akin to the extreme remedies which we often have heard spoken in folklore as "throwing out the baby with the bathwater". Change is one of life's constants but extreme change comes with a price and the receiver or the giver is going to be harmed one way or another. In the case of the Protestant Reformation, it was the church that bore the greatest suffering.

After eight hundred hours of clinical psychology training, I have come to understand that time and again the disruptions in our societies and institutions are often led by those who are from broken or dysfunctional homes and families. I know I will get some criticism for making this statement but many people are led by personal ambition in order to fill the void or a longing for the genuine love of a parent or mentor who can guide them through troubled waters. In Diarmaid MacColloch's book, *Christianity The First Three Thousand Years*, we read, "*it was not surprising that clerical and academic dynasties quickly grew up in Protestant Europe, and that thoughtful and often troubled, rather than self-conscious parsonage children took their place in a wider service. Such personalities as John and Charles Wesley, Gilbert and William Tenet, a trio of Bronte‡ novelists, Friedrich Nietzsche, Carl Jung, Karl Barth and Martin Luther King, Jr. took their restlessness and driven sense of duty into very varied rebuilding of Western society and consciousness, not all of which their parents might have applauded".*[144] As we can see in this quote, the author MacCulloch lists a group of activists that spans five hundred years of social and theological activism. This confirms the elements that the Roman Catholic priest and German monk Martin Luther faced in the late 1400's and early 1500's are not much different than the issues we face today with respect to our sense of duty and how our relationship with our earthly father affects our relationship with our Heavenly Father.

This transference is connected to our relationship to our Creator. If we have a meaningful and healthy relationship with our Heavenly Father, then we generally live a healthy and productive life. There is an old saying "the apple does not fall far from the apple tree". If it is a fruitful tree, then it is very possible the offspring will be fruitful as well. If the tree is fruitless then most likely the offspring will be unfruitful as well. Enter into the equation what was addressed in the previous short story that we need to be 'wired' or 'connected' to God. We will not realize our full potential until we "get connected" to the power source.

Many of our causes have substance and may be warranted but on a larger scale, they tend to lead to fragmented developments and undermine the foundations of our beliefs and culture because their value system is based on secular humanism. The later Caesars who became self-absorbed with their own indulgences and ambitions led to the fall of the Roman Empire. King Henry VIII led the Church of England away from the Roman Catholic Church because of his responsibility to provide a male heir for the kingdom. Separations do not always happen on a grand scale such as King Henry VIII. Even at the lower stratum there were thousands of nameless people whose influence led to the idolatry of a generation of people. In the most recent history of the nineteen fifties, sixties and seventies there were planted the seeds of the sexual revolution that led to

---

[144] Christianity First Three Thousand. (2010). *Christianity The First Three Thousand Years.* Viking. Published by Penguin Group, Penguin Group (USA), Inc. New York, New York. Diarmaid MacCulloch. Page 686.

the breakdown of the political, social, medical, governmental, legal and religious institutions.

In President John Fitzgerald Kennedy's famous statement from his 1961 inaugural address, he called for us to "ask not what your country can do for you, ask what you can do for your country".[145] I believe that President Kennedy saw a time when people were moving away from community service to self-service. He may not have known it at the time but he was certainly addressing the mounting growth of secular humanism. Years later we have the benefit of hindsight and I am afraid his clarion call was too little, too late. We have become a self-absorbed society and a nation of idolatry and greed. And in the religious area, it seems that every time someone has a different idea of theology or even a minor difference of opinion on how things should function, then a new church is born. Clergy find it difficult to admonish parishioners for fear of confrontation or reprisals. Our tried and true historical traditions and formulas have become sidelined to make way for the "latest and greatest" ways of worship. We should be more cautious when it comes to changing how we worship. The "latest and greatest" is not always the best answer to the yearning for a different worship service. More than likely it is a repackaging of a failed theology and practice. Change in the church should develop with great care.

Historically, then, we see that the first metamorphosis of the Christian Church occurred around 1000. The next metamorphosis came on the heels of the Protestant Reformation some five hundred years later. Out of this movement came the Magisterial Reformation[146] and the Radical Reformation[147]. Of the Magisterial

---

[145] President Kennedy. (2002). The American Heritage College Dictionary. *The American Heritage College Dictionary Fourth Edition.* Joseph P. Pickett, Vice President and Executive Editor. Published by the Houghton Mifflin Company. Boston, Massachusetts. Page 758.

[146] Magisterial Reformation. (2010). *Christianity The First Three Thousand Years.* Viking. Published by the Penguin Group. Penguin Group (USA), Inc. New York, New York. Diarmaid MacCulloch. Pages 622-653.

[147] Radical Reformation. (2010). *Christianity The First Three Thousand Years.* Viking. Published by the Penguin Group. Penguin Group (USA), Inc. New York, New York. Diarmaid MacCulloch. Pages 792-793.

Reformation, the Anglican Communion was formed in 1549 and has been in existence from that time of inception. The Anglican Communion is represented in America in the body of the Episcopal Church[148] which began after the American Revolution and was established in 1789 in Philadelphia, Pennsylvania. I mention this because the proponents of secular humanism are not limited to the religious arenas; they are writing or rewriting the histories of many of our institutions. A new Anglican Communion grew out of The Episcopal Church in 1979 when a revision of the Protestant Episcopal Book of Common Prayer was adopted followed by a newly revised hymnal in 1982. The Lutheran[149] denomination was created out of the Magisterial Reformation as well. From the Lutheran denomination evolved the Pietism movement around 1650. These Lutheran and Anglican denominations remain largely liturgical. Soon after the Anglican Communion was formed, the Puritan and Separatist denominations evolved around 1570. Out of the Puritan Movement evolved the Baptists around the turn on the 17th century. Next was organized the Southern Baptist denomination and then the Freewill Baptist denomination, and so on. Around 1725 was founded the Methodist[150] denomination which derives its name from the method of worship it practiced. It was led by John Wesley who ironically remained an Anglican priest until he died but never joined the Methodist denomination he founded. His brother Charles was also an Anglican priest and wrote many beloved hymns. The Adventist movement split from the Methodist denomination around 1825 and soon thereafter the Holiness movement began about fifteen years later around 1840.

---

[148] The Episcopal Church. (2001). Random House College Dictionary. *Random House Webster's College Dictionary 2nd Revised and Updated Edition*. New York, New York. www.randomhouse.com. Page 444.

[149] Lutheran. (2010). *Christianity The First Three Thousand Years*. Viking. Published by the Penguin Group. Penguin Group (USA), Inc. New York, New York. Diarmaid MacCulloch. Page 608.

[150] Methodist. (2010). *Christianity The First Three Thousand Years*. Viking. Published by the Penguin Group. Penguin Group (USA), Inc. New York, New York. Diarmaid MacCulloch. Page 795.

At the turn of the twentieth century developed the Pentecostal[151] movement which began out of the Holiness denomination.

Out of the Radical Reformation division of the Protestant Reformation sprang the Reformed Churches around 1570 or about the time the Anglican movement was forming. The Calvinist denomination began around 1580. Then in 1610, the Congregationalist split from the Presbyterian and Puritan denominations. And the splitting and the metamorphosis continue to this day. One can only wonder if and when the divisions and metamorphosis will end.

In perspective, at a recent clerical seminar, I learned that 34,000 independent churches are accounted for in the United States and growing. This number reflects all religions and denominations. There are about two dozen mainstream denominations, some that are previously mentioned, and include the Assemblies of God, the Disciples of Christ, the African Methodist Episcopal (AME), the Jehovah Witnesses, the Unitarian Church, the Congregationalist Holiness, the Brotherhood (Quakers), The Mennonites, the Church of Jesus Christ of Latter Day Saints (Mormon), and the Seventh Day Adventists to name a few. I mentioned these denominations because we can talk about them but to see them in writing drives home the argument that we are immensely divided. And then there are hundreds if not thousands of independent Christian churches with no allegiance to any denomination. Additionally, there are many books written on many other religions as well as cults and their apostasy. These other religions and cults will not be the focus of this book. Rather, I will address the theology and observance of Roman Catholic, Anglican, Eastern Orthodox, Lutheran, and Protestant Church history.

One cannot always place a finger on what motivates a person to begin a new church or denomination. The same things that motivated Martin Luther to initiate the Protestant Reformation will not be the same things that motivate us today. Not only

---

[151] Pentecostal. (2010). *Christianity The First Three Thousand Years.* Viking. Published by the Penguin Group. Penguin Group (USA), Inc. New York, New York. Diarmaid MacCulloch. Page 953.

did he have motivation from the relationship he had with his father, but apparently he had spent much of his time in the New Testament Book of Revelation. Although some of his best work was saved for his treatment of the Pauline Epistles. It seems part of his motivation was influenced by the ecclesiastical viewpoint of the end of time Scriptures, namely the Book of Revelation which was written by the Apostle John. He believed and proclaimed a view that the Roman Catholic Church was corrupted from within by an "internal anti-Christ" in the person of the Roman Catholic Pope. He also suggested that the Church was corrupted from the outside by an external anti-Christ or false prophet in the person of the Metropolitan or Patriarch of the Eastern Orthodox Church. This charge by Martin Luther has remained a recurring charge for hundreds of years. Every subsequent Pope has been charged by someone to be the anti-Christ. As a traditionalist, I can see that many things that were done wrong in the Protestant Reformation. On balance, I believe more right was done than wrong. For example one of the many benefits of the Protestant Reformation is that a system of checks and balances was instituted to safeguard against the misuse of power. However, disunity in the long run has hindered the growth and development of the Church and strengthens secular humanism.

Chapter Twelve

A Lay Perspective

"The curse of the Lord is in the house of the wicked: but he blesseth the habitation of the just. Surely he scorneth the scorners: but he giveth grace unto the lowly. The wise shall inherit glory: but shame shall be the promotion of fools".[152]

As an observer of history, my hope is that from this book, the reader may see more clearly what Christianity has experienced and may continue to experience over time. Christianity is constantly evolving and changing in application and practice and my primary concern is that when changes take place, they do not do so from a disagreement on dogma or doctrinal issues. Of course, the old adage that the "only constant in life is death and taxes" is a remark borrowed from Daniel Defoe in his book, *The Political History of the Devil, 1776* and reads, "things as certain as death and taxes, can be more firmly believed".[153] Change does occur if we like it or not. Doctrinal foundations in our Christian faith should be off-limits to reformers or those who are pushing for change for the sake of change. We should all affirm that our traditional practices and liturgical customs should not be available for change either. Now

---

[152] Holy Bible, The. (2004). The Holy Bible. *The Holy Bible Authorized King James Version.* World Publishing. Nashville, Tennessee. www.worldpublishing.com. The Old Testament. King Solomon. The Book of Proverbs 3:33-35. Page 291.

[153] Death and Taxes. (1776). Daniel Defoe. The Phrase Finder. *Nothing is certain but death and taxes.* www.phrases.org.uk.

over time there have always been suggestions to change the doctrine and dogma of the Church. As an example of changing doctrine, the hot topic today is the concerted effort in many denominations to admit homosexual men and women into the priesthood as well as to make same-sex unions acceptable under canon law. The thought of changing the church canons is a dangerous turn of events because any amendment to the canons of the church could cause a further splintering of the denomination and decline in its membership. In other words, the canons should not be treated like everyday laws which are repealed or enacted whenever there is a change in political party. Church canons should be treated like amendments to the US Constitution. Canons are based on sound doctrine and therefore should be very difficult to change.

Historically, the message of hope becomes more diluted and this is where we face a critical juncture. Frankly, when we abide by the tenets of secular humanism and not the tenets of sacred theism we place the fulfillment of God's complete measure of grace and knowledge at risk. We become, as I just read about in a news article, like a church in Atlanta now offering a drive-through service. Have we now reduced God to nothing more than something equivalent to fast food? Do we want God in a paper bag for takeout? Have we now compartmentalized God as we do in other areas of our lives as a time for this or a time for that? Well, God does not work that way. God is not and should not be a part-time God nor should He be at our beckoning call or disposal. This is what a secular humanist would wish. God should be to us as He was to Brother Lawrence--a fulltime God who lives with us 24/7 three hundred sixty-five days of the year. We have, in a sense, made religion or the practice of it, nothing more than entertainment for our instant gratification. The practice of religion is not a drive-through experience. It is a seven-course meal sitting at a table and being served by a priest or clergy. I believe that if we reach back and reclaim our Judeo-Christian heritage and recover these historical precepts and practices of the traditional faith of our fathers, then we can reclaim the depth of the Christian experience. However, we can take comfort in this lengthy process in that the author tells us in Hebrews chapter 13, that Jesus is the same *"yesterday and today, and forever"*.[154] For this reason, I offer this poem entitled Yesterday, Today and Tomorrow as a moment to meditate and replenish your soul.

> *"There are two days in every week about which we should not worry, two days which should be kept free from fear and apprehension. One of these days is Yesterday, with its mistakes and cares, its faults and blunders, its aches and pains. Yesterday has passed forever beyond our control. All the money in the world cannot bring back yesterday. We cannot undo a single act we performed; we cannot erase a single word we said. Yesterday is gone. The other day we should not worry about is tomorrow, with its possible adversities, its burdens, and its larger promise. Tomorrow is also beyond our immediate control. Tomorrow, the sun will rise, either in splendor or behind a mask of clouds, but it will rise. Until it does, we have no stake in tomorrow for it is as yet unborn. This leaves only one day today. Any man can fight the battles of just one day. It is only when you and I add the burdens of those two awful eternities. Yesterday and tomorrow, that we break down. It is not the experience of today that drives men mad. It is remorse or bitterness for something which happened yesterday and the dread of what tomorrow may bring. Let us therefore live but one day at a time"*. - Author Unknown[155]

---

[154] NIV Study Bible, The. (2011). The NIV Study Bible. *The Holy Bible, New International Version, NIV.* Published by Zondervan. Biblica, Inc. Grand Rapids, Michigan. Apollos, Barnabas or Paul. The Epistle of Paul to the Hebrews 13:8. Page 2085.

[155] Yesterday, Today and Tomorrow. (2012). *Yesterday, Today and Tomorrow.* Unknown Author. Anonymous. www.angelfire.com.

Around the end of the twentieth century, the Anglican Church and the Roman Church which had separated during the Protestant Reformation were on the threshold of making historical amends and perhaps finding full communion with each other. Regrettably, with the Roman Church not allowing women clergy as well as the consecration of homosexual and lesbian bishops into the Episcopal Church in America; combined with the revelation of pedophilia in the ranks of clergy in the Roman Church, the once warm reception became cold again. The ordination of a homosexual priest in the Protestant Episcopal Church in America gave fodder to those who opposed any cooperation or reconciliation between the Anglican and Roman Communions and opened old wounds that both Churches have had difficulty overcoming.

The Roman Catholic Church has yet to accept the viable consecration of English Bishop Matthew Parker[156] in the Anglican Church stating that his consecration was not valid because it only consisted of two bishops instead of three as canonically necessary. The canons of the Roman Catholic Church require three bishops to consecrate a new bishop, not two bishops. However, there were three bishops at Matthew Parker's consecration, but Rome would not accept one of the three bishops noting that he was not 'legitimate'. It seems that one of the three bishops at Parker's consecration had been consecrated by only two bishops therefore invalidating the consecration of Parker as the Canon Law requires. This type of disunity falls into the category of behavior, not the category of doctrine. And one would be hard pressed to prove that Rome was not splitting hairs on the issue. Do you think anyone would believe that Rome was not being spiteful or vengeful in light of the fact that they were losing a large contingent of believers in Great Britain and subsequently the colonies who, would then, contribute to the coffers? This perhaps worldly view is not included in this book to cause offense to anyone who has an opinion on either side. The Parker consecration happened several hundred years ago and it is time for the past to remain in

---

[156] Parker, Matthew. (2009). Encyclopedia Britannica. *Encyclopedia Britannica 2009 Deluxe Edition.* Chicago: Encyclopedia Britannica.

the past. It is my sincere hope and the hope of many Christians that we will someday see reconciliation between the parts of the Christian Church for there is one Savior Jesus Christ and one living God our Creator, and one Holy Spirit whom we worship. I would especially like to see the reconciliation of the twenty plus Anglican jurisdictions now in existence in the United States today. However, it is an understatement to say that any reconciliation of the Anglican Church and the Roman Church as well as the Orthodox Church will only strengthen the Christian Church. We certainly have enemies of Christianity around the world and we need to save our resistance for them rather than expending our negative energies toward each other.

There is an old saying that "all roads lead to Rome" and it is credited as an anonymous proverb. It is a historical fact that St. Peter was the first Bishop of Rome. Further, I understand from the Scripture that Jesus said, *"on this rock I will build my Church"*.[157] I also understand that the Bishop of Rome is often considered the greatest among equals. I know that St. Peter was Christ's first chosen Apostle. I commend the current Roman Catholic Pope Benedict XVI for the recent offering of an olive branch in the form of an Ordinariate to the Anglican Communion to reconcile past differences. I have read of the Pope making efforts to reconnect with the Eastern Orthodox Communion as well. To say that it would be a good day when the Pope of the Roman Catholic Church, the Patriarch of the Eastern Orthodox Church, and the Anglican Archbishop of Canterbury would make amends and extend full communion with each other is an understatement. One might think the earth's axis might swivel for a moment in time.

If we turn back the page, we can see that when Rome and Canterbury were on the verge of reconciliation, evil in the form

---

[157] Orthodox Study Bible, The. (2009). The Orthodox Study Bible. *The Orthodox Study Bible New King James Version.* St. Athanasius Academy Septuagint. Thomas Nelson Publishers. Thomas Nelson, Inc. Nashville, Tennessee. The New Testament. St. Matthew. The Gospel of Matthew 16:8. Page 1299.

of bad behavior exposes itself. Don't you think that Satan[158], who is called many other names such as Lucifer, the Devil, the Evil One, or the Antichrist to name a few, stands back with glee when he interrupts the mission of the Christian Church and causes it to engage in intramural warfare instead of engaging in spiritual warfare which the duty of the Church and is commissioned to do?

Several underpinnings of Christianity which take into account this intramural warfare have thus been diluted by the forces of secular humanism especially over the past fifty plus years and have been largely ignored by the leadership of the Christian denominations. For instance, some of these underpinnings or precepts are that: sin is real; that sin has consequences; that there is a price to pay for sin if one does not truly and earnestly repent and depart from the sin; that there is a real heaven; that there is one living God; that God has one Son and He is part of the Trinity. Some of the claims by secular humanists are that God is dead; that Mary was not a virgin; that Jesus was no more than a prophet; that the devil[159] is not real; that there are many ways to heaven; that we can live as we wish because we have been forgiven; that God is strictly a loving God and He will not pass judgment on us; and that hell is not real. Even the Time magazine cover in 1966 asked the question "is God dead"?[160] These are questions that undermine the core dogmas and doctrines of Christianity and the fact that they are treated as valid is a serious effort to misinform the people. And what makes matters worse is that many of the clergy are professing these apostasies. Of these issues we have a God-given choice to believe them or not. This is only possible because God created freedom of choice as a gift for us and we can exercise that freedom any way we wish. Therefore we can either believe that God is our

---

[158] Satan. (2010). *Christianity The First Three Thousand Years.* Viking. Published by the Penguin Group. Penguin Group (USA), Inc. New York, New York. Diarmaid MacCulloch. Page 687.

[159] Devil. (2011). Historical Theology. *A Companion to Wayne Grudem's Systematic Theology Historical Theology An Introduction to Christian Doctrine.* Zondervan. Grand Rapids, Michigan. Gregg R. Allison. Page 298-318.

[160] Time. (1966). *Time The Weekly Magazine.* Is God Dead? Cover. April 8, 1966. A publication of Time Warner Corporation. www.time.com.

Creator or not. We can believe that He is the only living God or not. We can believe in heaven or hell or not. Or we can believe in His only Son or not. And the list is endless because we have that freedom. But we also have consequences for our freedoms and one day we will have to pay for our choices. It is as simple as that. One day, and that day could be today, your choice will lead you in one direction or another.

So rather than reconcile, we have chosen to continue the debate over incidentals and through our behavior we fail to stay focused on the mission of the Christian Church to minister to the spiritual needs of the believers and the lost. If there was ever a time to seek reconciliation and unity in the Church, as well as to mend the broken-hearted, now it the time. Yesterday is gone and now a part of history and we cannot change that. But today we can do something about tomorrow. And now is a good time to start. Every day I see people yearning for the Gospel of our Lord and Savior Jesus Christ and to live out the precepts of sacred theism. Regretfully, these believers are not being fed as they should and the lost are being preyed upon by false doctrines and religions that offer a sense of community while espousing half-truths. My concern is that man who is searching for the real truth that only the Gospel of Jesus Christ can fulfill will be lost forever because we grapple with our institutional, behavioral, and turf issues. For these shortcomings may God forgive and have mercy on us.

Chapter Thirteen

Wired for God

"Hear, ye children, the instruction of a father, and attend to know understanding. For I give you good doctrine, forsake ye not my law".[161]

I mentioned in two previous short stories that we are wired to God. This is how God created us. In his book, *God Attachment*, Dr. Tim Clinton and Dr. Joshua Straub write that *"God wants to be in relationship with us, but when we sin we deliberately turn away from it"*.[162] The inner cravings we feel are where we are programmed by God to yearn for Him. Unfortunately, we typically fill this void with things of this world rather than the things of heaven. Here, again, we witness the secular humanism versus the sacred theism lifestyle. Ultimately we are spiritual beings that live in a body made of flesh. The Apostle Paul tells us how the flesh is in a constant state of war with the spirit. In St. Paul's Letter to the Galatians, we read,

> *"This I say then, walk in the Spirit, and ye shall not fulfill the lust of the flesh. For the flesh lusteth against the Spirit and the Spirit against*

---

[161] Holy Bible, The. (2004). The Holy Bible. *The Holy Bible Authorized King James Version*. World Publishing. Nashville, Tennessee. www.worldpublishing.com. The Old Testament. King Solomon. The Book of Proverbs 4:1-2. Page 291.

[162] God Attachment. (2010). *God Attachment, Why You Believe, Act, And Feel The Way You Do About God*. Howard Books, A Division of Simon & Schuster, Inc. New York, New York. Dr. Tim Clinton and Dr. Joshua Straub. Page 103.

the flesh; and these are contrary the one to the other: so that ye cannot do the things that ye would. But if ye be led of the Spirit, ye are not under the law. Now the works of the flesh are manifest, which are these; adultery (sexual intercourse with someone other than marriage partner), fornication (sexual intercourse outside of wedlock), uncleanness(foul or dirty mouth or body or moral evil[163]), lasciviousness (lust of the flesh), idolatry (blind or excessive devotion to something other than God), witchcraft (magic or sorcery), hatred (extreme dislike for one another), variance (saying one thing and doing another), emulations (imitate one another instead of God), wrath (vindictive anger), strife (bitter conflict), seditions (conduct and language inciting rebellion against authority), heresies (denial of religious doctrine), envying (feeling of resentment from the innate desire of another's property), murders (killing another human being), drunkenness (intoxicated of strong drink), reveling(extreme merrymaking), and such like: of the which I tell you before, as I have also told you in time past, that they which do such things shall not inherit the kingdom of God".[164]

Some of these are sins against God in the form of idolatry and witchcraft. Others are sins against man such as adultery, fornication, uncleanness, lasciviousness, hatred, variance, emulations, wrath,

---

[163] Believer's Bible Commentary. (1995). *Believer's Bible Commentary A Complete Bible Commentary in One Volume New King James Bible Version.* William MacDonald Edited by Art Farstad. Thomas Nelson Publishers, Inc. Nashville, Tennessee. St. Paul. Paul's Letter to the Galatians 5:20. Page 1894.

[164] Thompson Chain-Reference Bible. (2007). *Thompson Chain-Reference Bible King James Version.* B.B. Kirkbride Bible Company, Inc. Indianapolis, Indiana. The New Testament. St. Paul. Paul's Letter to the Galatians 5:16-21. Page 1238.

strife, seditions, heresies, and envying. Still others are against us such as drunkenness or revellings[165]. This is only a partial list. And you do not have to do all these things to be in contempt of God. It takes only one of these sins to be detrimental to your eternal salvation. If you are sincere in your repentance and turn away from this behavior, you will be washed anew in the Spirit. God loves a humble and contrite heart. Now, once you do this, the following is what you may expect. St. Paul continues as we read, *"but the fruit of the Spirit is love, joy, peace, longsuffering, gentleness, goodness, faith, meekness, temperance; against such there is no law. And they that are Christ's have crucified the flesh with the affections and lusts. If we live in the Spirit, let us also walk in the Spirit. Let us not be desirous of vain glory, provoking one another, envying one another"*.[166]

Now having said this, let me make a point about the direction our Christian Church is headed. Today, we find the symbols of Christianity becoming diluted or discarded. Secular humanism has caused us to view Christian symbols like the Bible or the Cross as unnecessary so therefore they are being replaced or packed away. Christian worship services have become more like concert halls holding pep rallies or rock concerts rather than a sanctuary where believers can worship with holiness and reverence. Now I do believe there is a place for this type of demonstration but I do not believe it is in a worship service or in a sanctuary. You might say we have crossed the line and merged all types of worship into a convoluted hodgepodge or cornucopia of ideas, desires, and opinions. The secular humanism agenda is designed to promote tolerance and uniformity and to make all things equal. Well, that is just not possible. God is not tolerant of sin, plain and simple. God does discriminate because you are either going to heaven

---

[165] Matthew Henry's Commentary. (1961). *Matthew Henry's Commentary in One Volume Zondervan Classic Reference Series.* Marshall, Morgan & Scott, Ltd. Zondervan. Grand Rapids, Michigan. Rev. Leslie F. Church. Page 1845.

[166] Thompson Chain-Reference Bible. (2007). *Thompson Chain-Reference Bible King James Version.* B.B. Kirkbride Bible Company, Inc. Indianapolis, Indiana.
The New Testament. St. Paul. Paul's Letter to the Galatians 5:22-26. Page 1238.

or you are going to hell. But where we end up is based on our choices, not God's. God does not tolerate sin and sin has a price that can only be paid in blood. If God did not uphold the law, and hold us accountable, then He would be a hypocrite and the law would be meaningless. And because God holds us to His high standard, this does not mean He hates us and ministers are not delivering hate-filled sermons when they preach the Gospel. They are not proclaiming a doctrine of hatred as proponents of secular humanism would like us to believe and neither should this cause ministers to be subject to hate crime prosecution.

Some seeds of disunity were planted in the Protestant Reformation when the liturgy was cast away by the radical reformers. In the void that followed was inserted, quite often, an abundance of music to fill the emptiness. Also, very lengthy sermons that repeatedly made the same point ensued as well as varying degrees of theatrics. Now we are supposedly improving the service again with rock and roll bands and allowing casual discussions while wearing casual dress as if we were attending a symposium or concert, not a worship service. The respect or reverence for God is missing because we now attend seminars instead of worship services. When this happens men are elevated, not God. God becomes diminished in man's eyes. Then we begin to hear the psychology of society rather than the theology of religion which is what we most need to hear. We need the substance of the Gospel and not the interpretation of our thoughts, feelings or emotions. We have replaced theology that is God-centered with psychology which is man-centered. Here, again, we witness the secular humanism versus the sacred theism, or evil versus good, or the flesh warring with the spirit. And we do not talk about sin or its consequences. Consequently, we are not taught to fear God as we should because we want our congregations to feel good about each other both corporately and individually.

My wife and I were talking recently about our education system. It seems every year we see our children graduate from one grade to another. In our day, we spent twelve years working for that one day when we graduated from high school. In my undergraduate years,

I had to wait four years to graduate. In my post graduate training, I had to study for seven years to receive my doctoral diploma. Now, it seems we graduate students from one year to the next year. Don't you think this diminishes the value and importance of an earned graduation and a sense of accomplishment? Have we reached the point that we need instant gratification in all that we do? The mentality of our educational system today seems to believe that it is more important to build your self-esteem rather than giving you the tools of general and specific knowledge and somehow that will make you a better person. That may be good advice because when you fail, then I guess you can feel better about failing because you will not be prevented from graduating. You might have made an F on your report card, but hey, at least you were able to graduate. And you might not be able to get a job or hold a job but there again, at least you graduated. However, this places us in a dilemma and this is one of the reasons I have written this book. It is time that we return to the traditional values and beliefs of our founding fathers. We could use a dose of traditional faith and practice the precepts of a life living the values of sacred theism. And we can do this by getting plugged into the source of our strength and getting rewired to God.

Again, I hope to give the reader the historical and timely foundations of the Christian faith so that when we are faced with the trials and temptations that we shall inevitably face, we will have that source of strength to undergird, strengthen, and empower us. An effort was made to keep the contents of this book as simple as possible. Developing a new theology or offering a new twist to an existing foundation or doctrine is not the aim of this book. I would rather provide a book that is easy to read and entertaining while being thoughtful and challenging rather than a book that will remain on a shelf gathering dust. This is another reason I created the new idiom, sacred theism. It is a way of life that is centered on God rather than centered on us as the secular humanist would have you believe and practice. These opposing forces are identified in each short story and solutions are offered to assist the Christian in his or her walk of faith. So much of what we believe as Christians has been trivialized and diluted. It is time to get back to the basics. One of my friends said to me recently, "let the theologians, seminarians, and professors debate the semantics of theology; give me something I can put to practical use". He went on to say, "as hard as I try, I cannot possibly understand what they are saying because of their level of training or education. Give me that old time religion that I can understand and I will be better off knowing how to live as a Christian". I can relate to my friend and his words were valuable to me. As a priest, I know I need to communicate to all levels with love and compassion and words that all can understand. Well, my friend asked for that old time religion, so now you have it and here it is. The battleground for our hearts and minds can be fought with the weapons you learn in this book. Keep this book as a companion to your Holy Bible and meditate on it to build your fortress in this difficult, challenging, and ever changing world.

Chapter Fourteen

The Moral Pendulum

"For I was my father's son, tender and only beloved in the sight of my mother. He taught me also, and said unto me, let thine heart retain my words; keep my commandments, and live".[167]

World War I and World War II in the last century had a more far reaching effect on this world than perhaps we will ever know. Certainly the world changed after Alexander the Great[168] conquered it before his death in 323 B.C. By his actions, he developed new trade routes that opened commerce and international trade. Then the Caesars[169] of the Roman Empire who ruled for over five centuries beginning in 27 B.C. had drastically changed the world as well. There is a saying that, "all roads lead to Rome" so that is where commerce flows as well as the culture of ideas. The Romans expanded on the trade routes that were developed by Alexander the Great. All wars have had their varying degrees of impact on

---

[167] Holy Bible, The. (2004). The Holy Bible. *The Holy Bible Authorized King James Version.* World Publishing. Nashville, Tennessee. www.worldpublishing.com. The Old Testament. King Solomon. The Book of Proverbs 4:3-4. Page 291.

[168] Alexander the Great. (2001). Random House College Dictionary. *Random House Webster's College Dictionary 2nd Revised and Updated Edition.* Random House, Inc. New York, New York. www.randomhouse.com. Page 32.

[169] Caesar, Julius. (2001). Random House College Dictionary. *Random House Webster's College Dictionary 2nd Revised and Updated Edition.* Random House, Inc. New York, New York. www.randomhouse.com. Page 718.

societies and institutions. Wars by nature accelerate change but WWII, the last Great War, is perhaps the game changer insofar as we are concerned because it affects us today. Many people believe the returning GI's[170] and sailors and marines who had grown up on the farms of rural America and the Bible Belt were exposed to many different cultures that were represented around the world. My friend and mentor, the Rev. Frederick Gough, a military historian noted that, "in addition to the horrors of war, the battlefield brought about a profound disillusionment in many of the returning servicemen and women. They were caused at best to question religion and at worst to discard it altogether. They thought God had let them down as they witnessed the failure of their government which was in chaos and their economies were in the tank. Therefore, they thought on whom they should depend? Their reply was that we depend on ourselves". And this was the foundation of secular humanism.

Many of those cultures believed in Gods other than the JudeoChristian God that we in America tended to worship, as did our founding fathers. To a degree, the worldly views of these cultures converged on an unsuspecting American citizenry. Various and conflicting cultural tastes were brought back with the returning GI's and sailors who fertilized the seeds of secular humanism in the late 1940's and early 1950's. These new seeds of secular humanism were broadcast to the winds and spread across America where they germinated and multiplied in the 1960's. And there seemed to be no firewall to stop the spread. But what had the most impact was not caused by the soldiers and sailors. It was the changing world. America was the preeminent industrial power in the world at that time period. When the manufacturing plants converted from a war footing providing massive war materials to a consumer footing providing consumer materials of every imagination, then the world changed forever. Factories retooled and provided material goods as had never been seen before. If you

---

[170] G.I. (2001). Random House College Dictionary. *Random House Webster's College Dictionary 2nd Revised and Updated Edition.* Random House, Inc. New York, New York. www.randomhouse.com. Page 552.

add into the mixture the psychology that soldiers and sailors now believed they were invincible, then you have a cocktail for secular humanism and its trappings. This is one of the main ingredients of secular humanism, a belief that man is greater than his world and that translates into a man who believes he is greater than his Creator. The conquering soldiers and sailors who returned home triumphant from the Pacific and Europeans theaters of operations fed the rise of materialism in America. Couple with the soldiers and sailors a society that had sacrificed and rationed for four long years and the need to reward them with material gain led to reckless consumerism. No institution, including the Church, saw what was developing right under their eyes. From the corporate boardrooms to the university classrooms, the seeds of change were being planted, nurtured, and they multiplied. The moral fabric of America was under siege and being challenged in a way as it never had been before. The pendulum of secular humanism had swung quickly away from the sacred theism that America had enjoyed since the founding of our nation in 1776.

America had indeed been founded upon the principles of sacred theism as it is evident in the Geneva Bible[171] written by Miles Coverdale and John Knox in 1560. Much of what was written in the US Constitution was taken from the precepts of the Geneva Bible and its successor the King James Bible in 1611. It was the Bible that arrived with the Puritans when our nation was founded. Additionally, the Scripture text found in the Anglican and Episcopal Book of Common Prayer until the 1979 edition is taken from the Geneva Bible, not the King James Bible, as many people believe. These principles are grounded in the principles of the Judeo-Christian values but that was beginning to change in the 20th century and in a big way.

---

[171] 1599 Geneva Bible, The. (2010) The 1599 Geneva Bible. *The 1599 Geneva Bible Patriot Edition The Holy Scriptures Contained in the Old and New Testaments.* Tolle Lege Press. White Hall Press. White Hall, West Virginia.

When post World War II materialism[172] began to take hold in this country, Americans found that they wanted more and more goods for themselves and their families. This constant and increasing appetite for more goods and services would contribute greatly to the undermining of our moral fabric. Materialism is centered on self and when self becomes greedy, then that which is desired becomes nothing more than idol worship in God's eyes. God created us to worship Him, not the things of this world. Excess materialism, for lack of a better term, is fool's gold and it traps people who ultimately find their lives nothing but an empty shell. If our material possessions matter, then when we die, why don't we take them with us to the next world? Not even the Pharaohs of Egypt who tried to take their possessions to the other world could do this. Now their precious possessions that they carried with them to their tombs in the Pyramids, if they have not rotted or turned to dust, reside in museums around the world. Remember that Christ Jesus said to the young rich man that it was easier for a camel to go through the eye of a needle that it was for a rich man to enter heaven. It must be an important lesson because the three Gospels of St. Matthew who recorded this passage in 19:24, St. Mark who recorded this passage in 10:25, and St. Luke who recorded this passage in 18:25 of the New Testament.

If we can push the moral pendulum back to the righteous way of life as exhibited by the principles of sacred theism, then it would be pleasing to God's eyes and our nation and world will become a better place to live. However, the snares of secular humanism are an aphrodisiac and their toxic effects on us are like drugs to an addict and nearly impossible to break. In this book, I commend Christians to seek God in the way of the traditional faith of our fathers. This would mean that we need to return to a sacred theism way of life putting God at the center of our lives instead of ourselves and our selfcentered materialism. This is a tall order since where we are today was centuries in the making. However, if we start the process

---

[172] Materialism. (2001). Random House College Dictionary. *Random House Webster's College Dictionary 2nd Revised and Updated Edition.* Random House, Inc. New York, New York. www.randomhouse.com. Page 818.

of returning to a God-centered society, quite frankly it will not take decades for it to mature and develop into a God-centered society and nation. Time and again it takes longer to build something than it take to dismantle it. But the task of returning the pendulum to the right is not as insurmountable as it may seem and for that we should not dismayed. Climbing a mountain takes one step at a time and before long we have conquered the mountain. Remember, we have God on our side and He is the one who created the mountain.

    We must begin the effort to turn our world in the direction of the God of Abraham, Isaac and Jacob. The alternative is too grim for us, our children and our grandchildren. If we do not, our descendents are looking at a life of bondage and slavery to secular humanism that has no place for sacred theism and for that matter is intolerant of anything that is represented by sacred theism. The future appears to be a life living in bondage where being ungrounded is the norm and morality becomes a word for the encyclopedia and the history books. The unchanged future will make Sodom and Gomorrah look like a Sunday afternoon picnic. If you need evidence, then go look at cable television, commercial television and the internet which displays no standards of public decency or behavior. They are becoming the garbage dump of society and the lack of morality and their influence on us is enormous. They are more like the side shows which were so popular at carnivals for anyone who dared to view them for their outrageous vice and sometimes horror. The only salvation on their part is that they were around only once a year at county fairs, but today's commercial and internet alternatives are around 24/7 three hundred and sixty-five days a year and the impact is saturating. The nature of the beast is to become more extreme to satisfy the growing appetite. Our communication media have desensitized us to ever more extreme sexual and violent behavior. More and more we are seeing children fall victim to all sorts of abuse and the abuse is becoming more frequent, more severe and more violent. Only a few years ago we would occasionally hear of parents killing their children, but now it seems to be a weekly occurrence. In Romans 6:19 NIV we read, *'I put this in human terms because you are weak in your natural selves. Just as you used to offer the parts of your body in slavery to impurity and to ever-increasing wickedness, so now offer them in slavery to righteousness leading to holiness".* In the end, God gives us a way out if we sincerely repent, choose righteousness, and live by His commandments.

Sociologists say the reason for this awareness is that we have more sources or communication tools to report abuse and therefore it seems to be out of control. I do not necessarily agree with this assessment. Neither does the Word of God. We are taught that the unbelievers are prone to increasing levels of violence. This dysfunctional behavior is directly related to the immoral and materialistic society we have become. Children and even domestic animals are not valued as God's creatures; rather they are treated like property or objects. Forty years of legalized abortion and tens of millions of deaths of unborn children have desensitized us as a society to the sacredness of human life. God will not look kindly on our nation if this trend continues. Abortion should be stopped for it is against the law of God.

Mao Tse-tung[173] used a tactic that was effective in his unification of mainland China while he overcame the legitimate government of the Republic of China. His successful tactic consisted of "two steps forward and one step back". When this tactic was implemented, people were pushed to the brink of collapse. Then forces eased off until they became familiar with their station in life. Then Chairman Mao would push two steps forward again and then ease off until people became accustomed to the situation. After numerous times of employing this tactic, Chairman Mao soon realized his initial objective. This continued until Chairman Mao had full control of China and he became a Communist[174] dictator.

---

[173] Mao Zedong. (2002). The American Heritage College Dictionary. *The American Heritage College Dictionary Fourth Edition.* Joseph P. Pickett, Vice President and Executive Editor. Published by the Houghton Mifflin Company. Boston, Massachusetts. Page 844.

[174] Communism. (2001). Random House College Dictionary. *Random House Webster's College Dictionary 2nd Revised and Updated Edition.* Random House, Inc. New York, New York. www.randomhouse.com. Page 269.

We should be aware that the proponents of secular humanism are using every tactic at their disposal to advance their cause at the expense of the majority of Americans who believe in sacred theism. For now, the majority of Americans seem to be against the marriage of same-sex individuals. However, last week Washington State approved the law that allows same-sex marriages and at this writing Maryland is considering following suit. There are now eight states which allow for this type of family structure and it is contrary to the traditional marriage as God designed for one man and one woman. The momentum is on the side of secular humanists to change not only social laws but church doctrine to include same-sex marriages in society. The building blocks and foundation of our society and the laws upon which they are based are grounded on the assumption that marriage is the union of one man and one woman and our laws have reflected this position until now. Proponents ask "what is a traditional marriage"? They are implying there is no such thing. As God tells us in the Scriptures, holy marriage is a triangular covenant between one man and one woman and Jesus Christ. However, many religious leaders have succumbed to the forces of secular humanism and have thrown the sanctity of holy matrimony under the bus, so to speak.

The forces of secular humanism have plotted and executed for decades the redefining of holy matrimony and family. Until now, the family unit consisted of one man and one woman or one father and one mother. Part of the effort to change this definition of family and marriage is to convince our society that this is how God created us. In order for secular humanists to prove God allowed same-sex marriage is to rewrite and reinterpret the Word of God. When supporters of homosexuality or the union of same-sex people as in two women or two men becomes the status quo; it must to be concluded by scientific evidence to become acceptable in society. This conclusion can be arrived from the medical and psychological communities who state that people are born this way because of their genetic makeup and therefore their behavior is normal. Then the proponents of same-sex marriage use the evidence from the scientific and medical communities to amend the policies of the educational and governmental communities; and these bodies incorporate their views into our books and have laws written to validate this belief into our systems including our religious community. As this happens, samesex marriages will become part of our social fabric. When this happens, it will be detrimental to our society and nation in the long run. It all depends on whose interpretation of Scripture is correct. If God is against it, then we will suffer. If God is for same-sex marriage, then we may be OK.

It is not just same-sex marriage that has the potential of undermining the foundation of our society. Abortion has been legal for over forty years and in that time period there have been over forty million babies murdered. This has had a negative effect on our society and has contributed to the desensitizing of us to the value of human life. Just imagine all the achievements that are lost from what could have been those future scientists, engineers, educators, communicators, and clergy. This, along with same sex-marriages, has caused a huge crack in the foundation of the traditional nuclear family. We have seen divorce become so easy to obtain that we now have a divorce rate of fifty percent. Many people ask, 'so why get married?' For this reason thousands upon thousands are living together out of wedlock. Here again, God will not look kindly on this condition. These are but some examples of two steps forward one step back. Where will it end? The choice is ours. Do we want the pendulum to swing back toward a society that honors the tenets of sacred theism; or, do we want it to continue toward a secular humanist society where Big Brother oversees our daily lives and we become objects of consumption and materialism rather than individuals who have life, liberty and freedom? If we live under the tenets of secular humanism, then we become enslaved in sin and bondage. If we live under the tenets of sacred theism, then we become enslaved in righteousness and remain free.

Chapter Fifteen

The Culture War

"Get wisdom, get understanding: forget it not; neither decline from the words of my mouth. Forsake her not, and she shall preserve thee: love her, and she shall keep thee".[175]

The Culture War is not easy to define, but we do know that it includes Christians who are under attack from every side. For this reason, Christianity as we know it is at a crossroads. For example, this morning I was listening to the MSNBC cable television program entitled UP with Chris Hayes who is an avowed liberal or one who is 'not limited to or by established, traditional, orthodox, or authoritarian attitudes, views, or dogmas.[176] He was talking about the Culture War.[177] In this 'war', according to Hayes, the

---

[175] Holy Bible, The. (2004). The Holy Bible. *The Holy Bible Authorized King James Version.* World Publishing. Nashville, Tennessee. www.worldpublishing.com. The Old Testament. King Solomon. The Book of Proverbs 4:5-6. Page 291.

[176] Liberal. (1979). The American Heritage Dictionary. *The American Heritage Dictionary of the English Language New College Edition.* William Morris, Editor. Published by the Houghton Mifflin Company. Boston, Massachusetts. Page 753.

[177] Culture War. (1960). Traditional/ Conservative versus Progressive/ Liberal or Christian vs. Non-Christian. www.answers.com/topic/culture-war.

polls indicate that those who consider themselves conservative[178] or 'those who tend to favor the preservation of the existing order and who regard proposals for change with distrust', are losing to those who consider themselves liberal. He cited a recent poll that indicates that for the first time in American history, the majority of Americans favor samesex marriages. To the traditional interpreter of the Scriptures, this is contrary to God's law and the doctrines of many Christian denominations. However, the trend seems to be changing in the leadership of many main stream denominations. Leaders of the Protestant Episcopal Church USA, the Presbyterian Church USA, and the United Methodist Church are pushing for an allowance of samesex unions by changing Church doctrine in their constitutions, canons, and bylaws. The Evangelical Lutheran Church in America has already adopted this policy of marrying same-sex individuals. In fact I read on the front page of the Morning News[179], a Florence, South Carolina based regional newspaper, an article entitled, "Culture Wars: They're Back".[180] Ironically, I do not believe they ever left us. The culture war is defined as "a clash of ideas...and a difference in the world viewpoints between believers and non-believers of Christ".[181] Thus, the culture war can be defined as the religious and social issues which affect the political, judicial, governmental, military, medical, ecclesiastical, and educational landscape of America. The underlying issue is the authority of Scripture in this culture war and three of the symptoms can be viewed as abortion, contraception and same-sex marriage. Many

---

[178] Conservative. (1979). The American Heritage Dictionary. *The American Heritage Dictionary of the English Language New College Edition.* William Morris, Editor. Published by Houghton Mifflin Company. Boston, Massachusetts. Page 284.

[179] Morning News. (February 12, 2012). *Morning News Sunday.* The Voice of the Pee Dee. A Media General Newspaper. Mark Blum Regional Publisher. www.scnow.com. Page 1A.

[180] Associated Press. (2012). *Culture Wars: They're Back Social Issues Overtake Politics in the U.S.* Morning News. A Media General Newspaper. Mark Blum Regional Publisher. www.scnow.com. Page 1A & 8A.

[181] Clash of Ideas, The. (2012). *The Clash of Ideas: The Culture War. Current News Affecting Your Freedom.* http://culture-war.info/.

issues of the culture war are bantered about in the political arena and are used regrettably as wedge issues. I believe social issues such as these already mentioned should be decided in church councils and assemblies, not in the political arena. Unfortunately, they are now a part of our social lexicon and our national political debate. For that reason these important social issues in my opinion do not get the attention or justice they deserve. More often than not, the opposing sides attack each other and demonize anyone with an honest viewpoint while characterizing them as intolerant, hate-filled, sexist, racist, greedy, self-centered, self-preserving and so on. Our debates no longer seem to be waged on the merits of an issue. Rather, the winner of our debates seems to be decided by whose vocal ability is the loudest or who has the greatest stamina. This type of language and characterization is not conducive to amicable solutions that are best for the parties who are involved. Social and political activists use these social issues as wedge issues to divide and conquer and they should be ashamed for ratcheting up the emotions of people for their own personal or political agenda. Again, these issues should be handled in God's court, not the court of public opinion. If this trend continues, we are approaching a day when we exchange our individual freedoms and allow Big Brother[182], like the character in George Orwell's famous novel *Nineteen Eighty-four*, to watch over us. We have thus yielded our personal responsibility to a government institution. If we become dependent on Uncle Sam[183] to provide for our social welfare and correct our social ills, then we are giving up too much freedom to a federal, state, or municipal government. One day, we may not be able to express our views in free speech. There are opponents of free speech who would actively prevent us from using the name Jesus Christ in public if they were given the chance. Consider, the Christmas season where we find that many refer to Christmas

---

[182] Orwell, George. (2009). Encyclopedia Britannica. *Encyclopedia Britannica 2009 Deluxe Edition*. Chicago: Encyclopedia Britannica.

[183] Uncle Sam. (2001). Random House College Dictionary. *Random House Webster's College Dictionary 2nd Revised and Updated Edition*. Random House, Inc. New York, New York. www.randomhouse.com. Page 1421.

as Xmas. However, there is a minority who views the omitting of Christ from Christmas, and sees the X as the Greek letter for Christos; therefore they may not think that Christ is being omitted. Additionally, we see in many places during the season where we can no longer construct a Christmas tree or nativity scene on public property even on a temporary basis.

In any event, the trend for losing our religious and cultural freedoms is well underway and we will have to live with political parties using social issues to prod the electorate in whichever direction they wish to lead. Unfortunately, this trend is undermining the foundations of our society as a corporate entity. Far too many politicians are in office serving their own needs and passing laws they do not have to obey. For instance, the Congress is not subject to Occupational Health and Safety Administration regulations. This current structure leaves no room for a sacred institution to adequately serve the needs of a society. Individual relationships where people get involved are the most successful and this is why social and civic organizations at the local level are the most effective. The government is too insular and too far removed from the individual to adequately manage the needs of that person. Managing from an ivory tower is not the best way.

The seeds of the cultural war were planted several decades ago and are harvested in the principles and precepts of secular humanism. They have been nurtured at our universities and colleges where those who lead this battle are insulated by the ivy-covered fortresses wherein they plot and they have no checks and balances because they are generally accountable only to their colleagues. It is equal to the fox guarding the henhouse. If anyone gets out of line, they are coaxed back into alignment without any tangible penalty or sacrifice. This is true of many government agencies as well. Graduates of these liberal colleges and universities have now entered into and become managers of business and media organizations which continue to embrace the ideals of secular humanism. They market them to a society which used to be overwhelmingly against them. Secular humanism has permeated to such an extent that as Chris Hayes said on his February 11, 2011 news show, the liberal class has become the majority in America.

The culture war may not use guns and bullets but its effect seems greater. It is more like a smart bomb that takes out individuals and leaves all structures in place. The culture war is no less intense than that of any military operation but is it more effective because it attacks the hearts and minds of society. Therefore it has a long range effect. The culture war is the most important war our country has ever been engaged. If the forces of secular humanism succeed, then our country will be weakened and we will be subject to outside forces or enemy nations who wish to conquer us. The stakes are high and we must pay attention, be on guard and remain vigilant. We must strengthen our fortresses and prepare for a long and protracted battle. We must do so because we have no other choice. The lessons of the Roman Empire and its ultimate demise are grounded in secular humanism. America is cut from the same cloth so we should take stock of the Roman experience lest we forget and fall into the same demise. We are quickly heading down the same path as the Romans but we have time to reverse the trend. Secular humanism is not the answer and neither is it the cure.

It is time to turn this situation around and get on our knees and pray for reconciliation and forgiveness. I fear that our corporate and individual sins are weighing heavily on the trusses of this once JudeoChristian nation. One wonders how long these supports will hold up under the heavy pressure. In the Old Testament, time and again we read of the pendulum swinging between secular humanism and sacred theism. Ultimately the societies who idolize the tenets of secular humanism and the materialism it spawns fall under their own weight. The survivors are those societies and nations who live by the tenets of sacred theism.

Chapter Sixteen

Sacred Theism vs. Secular Humanism

"Wisdom is the principal thing: therefore get wisdom: and with all thy getting get understanding. Exalt her, and she shall promote thee: she shall bring thee to honour, when thou dost embrace her. She shall give to thine head an ornament of grace: a crown of glory shall she deliver to thee. Hear, O my son, and receive my sayings: and the years of thy life shall be many".[184]

In this last short story of Part One, it occurred to me that I may need to expound on the opposing views of secular humanism versus sacred theism before we continue to Part Two of this book. Secular humanism has been a part of our social lexicon for the last century. I created sacred theism, a new idiom, because there was no other phrase that adequately projected the theme of what the combination of these two words mean. In the following paragraphs, you will read the interpretations and meanings of both sacred theism and secular humanism. Your understanding will depend on your ability to grasp the concepts portrayed in this

---

[184] Holy Bible, The. (2004). The Holy Bible. *The Holy Bible Authorized King James Bible Version.* World Publishing. Nashville, Tennessee. www.worldpublishing.com. The Old Testament. King Solomon. The Book of Proverbs 4:7-10. Page 292.

chapter. Sacred theism is one of the key ingredients in this book. This book's short stories are intended to be entertaining as well as informative. I hope the subject matter in this book keeps the reader engaged because I believe it is vitally important to our future as Jews and Christian people as well as our society, nation and world.

Secular is defined as worldly, while humanism is defined as man. Sacred is defined as heavenly, while theism is defined as Father. Secular humanism represents the worldly man while sacred theism represents the Heavenly Father. Secular humanism is the doctrine of a man-centered world that manifests itself in such material things as cars, boats, trucks, clothes, shoes, jewelry, housing, entertainment, vacations, sports, or all things that feed the human flesh and cause hatred, envy, jealously, contempt, pride and so on. In contrast, sacred theism is the doctrine of a God-centered world that praises, adores, worships, and follows the commandments of God and is represented in all spiritual virtues such as faith, belief, grace, trust, salvation, humility, care, concern, hope, commitment, discipline, wisdom, understanding, knowledge, love, peace, joy, happiness and all such things that feed the human spirit.

There are two 'isms' which have similar meanings. Deism and theism both refer to God. The difference is that deism refers to a god who is unattached to His creation, while theism refers to our God who is attached to his creation. In sacred theism, we not only have a Holy God or Heavenly Father but we have a God who is actively involved in everyone's lives. God requires us to seek Him through His Son Jesus Christ and eventually to have a personal relationship with Him.

Sacred means holy while deism means natural as in the world God created. It is not taken in the sense of pantheism or the worship of "Mother Nature".[185] Mother Nature is personified as a being. This false premise leads us in the wrong direction. However, it demonstrates how easily one can get distracted or journey in

---

[185] Mother Nature. (2001). Random House College Dictionary. *Random House Webster's College Dictionary 2nd Revised and Updated Edition*. Random House, Inc. New York, New York. www.randomhouse.com. Page 865.

the wrong direction. In the world we live in today, we are seeing the convergence of world religions claiming such falsehoods as all gods are one in the same; or that Jesus was just like Muhammad, a prophet; or there are many ways to heaven. Anyone who claims these falsehoods are either ignorant, foolish or presumably an atheist. Remember the first of the Ten Commandments, "thou shalt have no other gods before me". You will read more about this in the first section of Part Two.

If your life is built on materialism or secular humanism, then you will ultimately live in an empty world. What you acquire will quickly lose its luster and shine and in a few months you will have discarded the item for a newer one or you will be looking for another "new" thing that will feed that insatiable desire. Each time you will soon realize that the nova of the new thing is short lived. If you recall the earlier short story entitled *Wired for God*, I wrote about the Scripture verses in Galatians which identify the opposing sides. It is worth repeating in an abbreviated version. A life devoted to secular humanism will lead to one or more of the following: adultery, fornication, uncleanness, lasciviousness, idolatry, witchcraft, hatred, variance, emulations, wrath, strife, seditions, heresies, envying, killings, drunkenness, reveling and so forth. However, if you seek the tenets of sacred theism you will experience one or more of the following: love, joy, peace, longsuffering, gentleness, goodness, faith, meekness, temperance, knowledge, wisdom, discipline, humility, forgiveness and so forth.

As I write this book and contemplate its impact, in the back of my mind, I am preparing to be ridiculed and chastised by the forces of evil that are roaming about like the roaring lion.[186] We read about these forces in the New Testament and they are out to devour us. As we read in I Peter, "*8 be sober, be vigilant; because your adversary the devil walks about like a roaring lion, seeking whom he may devour. 9 Resist him, steadfast in the faith, knowing that the*

---

[186] Believer's Study Bible, The. (1991). The Believer's Study Bible. *The Believer's Study Bible New King James Version*. Thomas Nelson Publishers. Nashville, Tennessee. The New Testament. St. Peter. The first Book of Peter 5:8-11. Page 1772.

same sufferings are experience by your brotherhood in the world. 10 but may the God of all grace, who called us to His eternal glory by Christ Jesus, after you have suffered a while, perfect, establish, strengthen, and settle you".

Therefore, anyone who stands for what is righteous, sacred, and true will find themselves under constant condemnation and scurrilous attacks. I must advise you to develop a thick skin for if you decide to follow Christ, you too will be crucified, not necessarily in the flesh but emotionally and spiritually. God will protect us from the attacks of the evil that surrounds us and we will live a joyous life. No doubt, when we pray to our Heavenly Father we enter into spiritual warfare. God will sustain us as long as we are prepared by applying His teachings which we learned in the Holy Scriptures. If we do not learn Biblical precepts, we are like an unprotected lamb. We must be brave and remain steadfast in our faith. How much more the reward if we have the courage to take a stand for Christ Jesus? I pray this book offers hope and strength to those who seek the help it provides. It can help us to prepare for the battles that are yet to be fought. For this reason, I also commend to you the Holy Bible and implore you to put on the "armor of God."[187] I would be remiss not to steer you in the direction of the armory of God. The full armor of God is found in the book of Ephesians and is described as follows:

> *"10 Finally, my brethren, be strong in the Lord and in the power of His might. 11 Put on the whole armor of God that you may be able to stand against the wiles of the devil. 13 For we do not wrestle against flesh and blood, but against principalities, against powers, against the rulers of the darkness of this age, against spiritual hosts of wickedness in the heavenly places. 13*

---

[187] Believer's Study Bible, The. (1991). The Believer's Study Bible. *The Believer's Study Bible New King James Version.* Thomas Nelson Publishers. Nashville, Tennessee. The New Testament. St. Paul. Paul's Letter to the Ephesians 6:10-18. Page 1683.

> *Therefore take up the whole armor of God, that you may be able to withstand in the evil day, and having done all, to stand. 14 Stand therefore, having girded your waist with truth, having put on the breastplate of righteousness. 15 And having shod your feet with the preparation of the gospel of peace; 16 above all, taking the shield or faith with which you will be able to quench all the fiery darts of the wicked one. 17 And take the helmet of salvation, and the sword of the Spirit, which is the word of God; 18 praying always with all prayer and supplication in the Spirit, being watchful to this end with all perseverance and supplication for all the saints".*

This Scripture lesson is invaluable as we travel through life with all its pitfalls that often come without warning. God will protect us, but we have to do our part as well. In the final analysis, we are engaged in a cosmic battle of evil (secular humanism) versus good (sacred theism). We have a choice to make either for one side or the other. There is not a middle ground. It is that simple. In the Didache we read, "there are two ways, one of life and one of death, and there is a great difference between the two ways".[188] I pray you make the choice for good and muster the discipline and forbearance to stay on the side of sacred theism.

---

[188] Didache, The. (2010). The Didache. *The Didache A Window on the Earliest Christians.* SPCK. Baker Academic. A Division of Baker Publishing Group. www.bakeracademic.com. Grand Rapids, Michigan. Thomas O'Loughlin, Editor. Page 160.

PART TWO
Christian Core Beliefs

Chapter Seventeen

The Decalogue and Two Commandments

The Decalogue is more easily recognized as the *Ten Commandments*[189] which God gave to Moses on Mt Sinai. They are recorded in two books of the Old Testament, namely Exodus and Deuteronomy. These books are the second and fifth books of the Holy Bible. They are also known as the *Torah* or the *Pentateuch*[190] for those of the Jewish faith. The Decalogue represents God's covenant with his chosen people, the Israelites or Jewish people. God's new covenant is found in the New Testament and it establishes His covenant with both Jews and Gentiles alike, whereas the first covenant affected only the Jews. The Ten Commandments represent the moral foundation for Judaism and subsequently for Christianity. They are the first written set of rules or laws which God established with mankind. They are considered to be a moral guideline for His people and how He expects them to live. The Israelites had grown from the twelve sons of Jacob, Leah and her maidservant Zilpah, and Rachel and her maidservant Bilhah into a nation during their captivity in Egypt. The sons of

---
[189] Ten Commandments. (2010). *Christianity The First Three Thousand Years.* Viking. Published by the Penguin Group. Penguin Group (USA), Inc. New York, New York. Diarmaid MacCulloch. Page 61.
[190] Pentateuch. (2010). *Christianity The First Three Thousand Years.* Viking. Published by the Penguin Group. Penguin Group (USA), Inc. New York, New York. Diarmaid MacCulloch. Page 54.

Leah were Rueben, Simeon, Levi, Judah, Issachar, and Zebulun. The sons of Rachel were Joseph and Benjamin. The sons of Bilhah were Dan and Naphtali and the sons of Zilpah were Gad and Asher. The nation of Israel was led out of Egypt by God and entered into "a land flowing with milk and honey".[191] Now it was time for God to establish some ground rules with His chosen people and the Ten Commandments was the expression of His covenant.

The first recording of the Ten Commandments is found in Exodus 20:3-17 and the second recording is found in Deuteronomy 5:7-21. God writes the commandments over the course of forty days and gives them to Moses, His chosen leader of the Jewish people. As the forty days unfolded, Moses climbed up the mountain to the pinnacle of Mt. Sinai where he meets with God in a dense fog or cloud. God wrote with His finger on two stone tablets His Ten Commandments. When Moses returned to his people with the two tablets, he saw Aaron, his brother, and the Israelites engaging in immoral and sinful behavior and it so angered him that he broke the original two tablets. Two sins do not make things right so God had Moses chisel a second set of stone tablets with his own hands. It is not evident where the modern location of Mt. Sinai is but many geologists and ancient historians believe the location could also be Mt. Horeb. The following two versions of the Ten Commandments are provided for comparison. They are as follows from the King James Version:

Exodus 20:3-17 Version[192]

> *"3 Thou shalt have no other gods before me. 4*
> *Thou shalt not make unto thee any graven image,*
> *or any likeness of anything that is in heaven above,*
> *or that is in the earth beneath, or that is in the*
> *water under the earth: 5 thou shalt not bow down*

---

[191] Thompson Chain-Reference Bible. (2007). *Thompson Chain-Reference Bible King James Version*. B.B. Kirkbride Bible Company, Inc. Indianapolis, Indiana. The Old Testament. Moses. The Book of Exodus 3:8. Page 66.

[192] Today's Parallel Bible. (2000). *Today's Parallel Bible NIV NASB Updated KJV NLT*. Zondervan Publishing House. The Zondervan Corporation. www.zondervan.com. Grand Rapids, Michigan. The Old Testament. King James Version. Moses. The Book of Exodus. Pages 168-170.

thyself to them, nor serve them: for I the Lord thy God am a jealous God, visiting the iniquity of the fathers upon the children unto the third and fourth generation of them that hate me: and showing mercy unto thousands of them that love me, and keep my commandments. 7 Thou shalt not take the name of the Lord thy God in vain; for the Lord will not hold him guiltless that taketh his name in vain. 8 Remember the Sabbath day, to keep it holy. 9 Six days shalt thou labour, and do all thy work; 10 but the seventh day is the Sabbath of the Lord thy God; in it thou shalt not do any work, thou, nor thy son, nor thy daughter, thy manservant, nor thy maidservant, nor thy cattle, nor thy stranger that is within thy gates; 11 for in six days the Lord made heaven and earth, the sea, and all that in them is. And rested the seventh day wherefore the Lord blessed the Sabbath day, and hallowed it. 12 Honour thy father and thy mother; that thy days may be long upon the land which the Lord thy God giveth thee. 13 Thou shalt not kill. 14 Thou shalt not commit adultery. 14 Thou shalt not steal. 16 Thou shalt not bear false witness against thy neighbor. 17 Thou shalt not covet thy neighbor's house; thou shalt not covet thy neighbor's wife, nor his manservant, nor his maidservant nor his ox, nor his ass, nor any thing that is thy neighbor's".

Deuteronomy 5:7-22 Version[193]

"7 Thou shalt have none other gods before me. 8 Thou shalt not make thee any graven image, or

---

[193] Today's Parallel Bible. (2000). *Today's Parallel Bible NIV NASB Updated KJV NLT.* Zondervan Publishing House. The Zondervan Corporation. www.zondervan.com. Grand Rapids, Michigan. The Old Testament. King James Version. Moses. The Book of Deuteronomy 20:7-22. Pages 412-414.

any likeness of anything that is in heaven above, or that is in the earth beneath, or that is on the waters beneath the earth; 9 thou shalt not bow down thyself unto them nor serve them; for I the Lord thy God am a jealous God, visiting the iniquity of the fathers upon the children unto the third and fourth generation of them that hate me, 10 and showing mercy unto thousands of them that love me and keep my commandments. 11 Thou shalt not taketh the name of the Lord thy God in vain; for the Lord will not hold him guiltless that taketh his name in vain. 12 Keep the Sabbath day to sanctify it, as the Lord thy God hath commanded thee. 13 Six days thou shalt labour, and do all thy work; 14 but the seventh day is the Sabbath of the Lord thy God; in it thou shalt not do any work, thou, nor thou son, nor thy daughter, nor thy manservant, nor thy maidservant, nor thine ox, nor thine ass, nor any of thy cattle, nor thy stranger that is within thy gates; that thy manservant and maidservant may rest as well as thou; 15 And remember that thou was a servant in the land of Egypt, and that the Lord thy God brought thee out thence through a mighty hand and by a stretched out arm: therefore the Lord thy God commanded thee to keep the Sabbath day. 16 Honour thy father and thy mother as the Lord thy God hath commanded thee; that thy days may be prolonged, and that it may go well with thee, in the land which the Lord thy God giveth thee. 17 Thou shalt not kill. 18 Neither shalt thou commit adultery. 19 Neither shalt thou steal. 20 Neither shalt thou bear false witness against thy neighbor. 21 Neither shalt thou desire thy neighbour's wife. Neither shalt thou covet thy neighbour's house, his field, or his manservant, or his maidservant, his ox, or his ass, or anything that is thy neighbour's".

As we can see there is very little substantive difference in the two versions of the Ten Commandments. These commandments are vitally important to all Christians and Jews alike. They are the foundations of our relationship with God and our fellow man. They have been the foundations of Judeo-Christian laws throughout history. Many of man's laws can be traced back to the principles found in the Ten Commandments. Therefore, these commandments should be some of the first lessons we learn as Christians. This is why I have included them in the first segment of Part Two. In the Anglican Book of Common Prayer we are led by the rubrics to conduct a responsive reading of the Ten Commandment every month. This monthly restatement provides a reminder and builds a solid foundation on which to grow in our fellowship with God. In summary, they declare God to be the one and only true and living God, who forbids any idol worship, and promises punishment for anyone who does not love Him or blasphemy His name. He also commands us to observe the Sabbath as Holy and forbids us to do any work on that day while honoring our parents, forbidding murder, adultery, theft, false witness, or covetousness. Learning the tenets of the Ten Commandments is an ideal place to start when developing a lifestyle or regimen of sacred theism.

The next lesson we should learn is found in the New Testament and is known as the *Summary of the Law*[194]. The *Summary of the Law* is given by Jesus to His disciples and it explains the Ten Commandments and ties them together as a fundamental foundation of both Judaism and Christianity. If you read the Ten Commandments, then you will soon realize that the first four commandments apply to man's relationship with God and the last six commandments pertain to man's relationship with each other. To fully understand and comprehend the meaning, I have included the *Summary of the Law* as follows:

---

[194] Thompson Chain-Reference Bible. (2007). *Thompson Chain-Reference Bible King James Version*. B.B. Kirkbride Bible Company, Inc. Indianapolis, Indiana. The New Testament. St. Matthew. The Gospel according to St. Matthew 22:36-40. Page 1041.

> "Master, which is the great commandment in the law? Jesus said unto him, 'Thou shalt love the Lord thy God with all thy heart, and with all thy soul, and with all thy mind. This is the first and great commandment. And the second is like unto it. Thou shalt love thy neighbor as thyself. On these two commandments hang all the law and the prophets'".

Jesus was often looked upon in his day as the second Moses or the Messiah who was predicted by the prophets in the Old Testament. He was come to deliver God's chosen people from their bondage to the Romans. Therefore, it is fitting that He gave us the Summary of the Law as the 'second' Moses while the first Moses gave us the Ten Commandments. Now if we examine this further, we soon realize that it was not really Moses that gave us the Ten Commandments; it was God. Moses was the intermediary. So God gave man his first written covenant, the Ten Commandments. If we believe in the Trinity of God the Father, God the Son, and God the Holy Spirit, then God, in the form of Jesus, gave us his second covenant as summarized His version of the law, quoting from Deuteronomy 6:5 and Leviticus 19:18.

Therefore, we read in the New Testament's *Summary of the Law*, the first and great commandment is about our relationship with God our Heavenly Father, and the second great commandment is about our relationship with each other. Both of these two commandments are grounded in the word love. Why love, you may ask? Love is inherent because God is love. The Apostle John wrote in his first epistle that, "*he that loveth not, knoweth not God; for God is love*"[195]. God defines love for He created it. God is love and love is God. Therefore when we say to one another, "I love you", we are saying 'God loves you". And there is a difference between "I lust you" and "I love you". Lust is of the flesh and love is of the

---

[195] Thompson Chain-Reference Bible. (2007). *Thompson Chain-Reference Bible King James Version*. B.B. Kirkbride Bible Company, Inc. Indianapolis, Indiana. The New Testament. St. John. The first epistle of I John 4:8. Page 1298.

spirit. This is a great example or contrast between sacred theism and secular humanism. Secular is of the flesh and sacred is of the spirit. There is no better way to describe our relationship with our Creator. Our Heavenly Father loved His greatest creation, man, so much that He sacrificed His only Son that we might have salvation and the opportunity to live eternally with Him in heaven. His Son, Jesus Christ the righteous is the propitiation or perfect offering for our sins. God would accept no other sacrifice for all mankind's sins other than the sacrificial blood of His Son. Therefore, the entire Word of God, from Genesis to Revelation, is the greatest love story ever written and no Hollywood film can match it. It centers on the unconditional love that our Father feels for His greatest creation, man. No wonder we read that God created man in His own image. If we follow the lessons of the Ten Commandments and the Summary of the Law, then we will find ourselves in good stead with our Heavenly Father and our place in eternity with Him and Christ Jesus will be secured if we repent of our sins and place our faith in God's love. If we do not depart from a life that is full of indulgences in the vices of secular humanism, then I predict our destiny will be through the gates of hell. There are many sources of study but for a detailed account of the Decalogue, may I suggest the *Catechism of the Catholic Church*[196]. There you will receive more instruction than in most other sources.

---

[196] Catechism of The Catholic Church. (1995). *Second Edition Catechism of the Catholic Church Revised in Accordance with The Official Latin Text Promulgated By Pope John Paul II.* Published by Doubleday. A Division of Random House, Inc. New York, New York. Pages 551-672.

Chapter Eighteen

The Three Primary Creeds

There are three primary creeds written for the Christian faithful. They are the Apostles Creed, The Nicene Creed, and the Athanasian Creed with minor variations. There are other creeds, but these are the three most adhered to in Christianity. There are many more creeds or statements of belief and several denominations use these other various statements which they have learned to love and have incorporated them in their worship services. Additional creeds or statements of belief include the Creed of Chalcedon, the First Confession of Basle (1534), Zwinglian (Swiss) Confessions, the Reformed Confessions, The Form of Concord (1577), The Augsburg Confession (1530), Luther's Catechisms (1529), The Confessions of Gennadius (1453), The Orthodox Confession or the Catechism of Peter Mogilas (1643), to name a few.

Creeds or statements of belief began as a way to proclaim with the mouth what the heart held in abundance. "The Church is, indeed, not founded on symbols, but on Christ: not on any words of man, but on the Word of God; yet it is founded on Christ as confessed by men, and a creed is man's answer to Christ's question, man's acceptance and interpretation of God's word."[197] The authorities of the creeds are found in the Holy Scriptures as the only infallible truth on Christian practice as it applies to faith. Therefore, "the Bible is the Word of God while the creeds and confessions are man's answer to God's Word. The Bible is the rule of faith, the Creed is the rule of doctrine, and the Bible is the divine absolute while the confession is 'only an ecclesiastical and relative authority'".[198]

So let us first review the definition of a creed. A creed is defined in the American Heritage Dictionary as: "1. a formal statement of religious belief; confession of faith. 2. an authoritative statement of certain articles of Christian faith that are considered essential. 3. a statement of belief, principles, or opinions".[199] Creeds then verbalize in words and in written form our thoughts, ideals and beliefs. Their value is held in that they are summaries of the doctrines of the Church and the Holy Scriptures. They provide a means to strengthen the bonds of believers as well as aid in the understanding of the Bible. They offer helpful hints for the instruction of children in the form of the Catechism for instance. They, of particular importance, hinder the development of false doctrine, heresy and practice.

There are many pressures on the doctrine and practice of the Christian Church. On that premise, I consciously chose to summarize the views of Christendom in the three primary Christian creeds rather than pick them apart and dissect them to no end. If

---

[197] Creeds of Christendom, The. (2007). *The Creeds of Christendom With a History and Critical Notes Volume I The History of Creeds.* Baker Books. Written by Philip Schaff. Revised by David S. Schaff. A Division of Baker Book House Company. Grand Rapids, Michigan. Page 5.

[198] Creeds of Christendom, The. (2007). *The Creeds of Christendom With a History and Critical Notes Volume I The History of Creeds.* Baker Books. Written by Philip Schaff. Revised by David S. Schaff. A Division of Baker Book House Company. Grand Rapids, Michigan. Page 7.

[199] American Heritage Dictionary, The. (1979). The American Heritage Dictionary. *The American Heritage Dictionary of the English Language New Heritage Edition.* William Morris, Editor. Published the by Houghton Mifflin Company. Boston, Massachusetts. Page 311.

properly used, this book could be a helpful companion to the Holy Scriptures. Over the centuries these creeds have been hashed and rehashed and reinterpreted numerous times and in various ways. I understand the reason for questioning the relevancy as well as the doctrine because they need to be able to stand on their own and the test of time. And to their credit they have successfully passed the criticism. These creeds are an excellent follow-up to the Decalogue and Summary of the Law because they will begin to develop in thought and Word the meaning of God's commandments as He deemed in His two covenants with man. Needless to say, they are instrumental to laying the foundation and practice of a life of sacred theism.

Therefore, they are presented in their entirety in the order in which they were written although it is difficult to believe that the Nicene Creed, as history shows, is written before the Apostles Creed. We have always assumed that the Apostles Creed was written or at least contributed to by the Apostles. Its date of creation does not support this often believed assumption.

The Nicene Creed[200] *(325AD)*

> *I believe in one God the Father Almighty, Maker of heaven and earth, And of all things visible and invisible; And in one Lord Jesus Christ, the only begotten Son of God, Begotten of His Father before all worlds, God of God, Light of Light, Very God of very God; Begotten, not made; Being of one substance with the Father. By whom all things were made. Who for us men and for our salvation came down from heaven, And was incarnate by the Holy Ghost of the Virgin Mary,*

---

[200] Creeds of Christendom, The. (2007). *The Creeds of Christendom With a History and Critical Notes Volume I The History of Creeds.* Baker Books. Edited by Philip Schaff. Revised by David S. Schaff. A Division of Baker Book House Company.
Grand Rapids, Michigan. Pages 27-29.

And was made man; And was crucified also for us under Pontius Pilot, He suffered and was buried, And the third day he rose again according to the Scriptures. And ascended into heaven, And sittith on the right hand of the Father. And He shall come again, with glory to judge both the quick and the dead; whose kingdom shall have no end. And I believe in the Holy Ghost, the Lord, and Giver of Life, Who proceedeth from the Father and the Son, Who with the Father and the Son together is worshipped and glorified, Who spake by the Prophets. And I believe in one Catholic and Apostolic Church. I acknowledge one Baptism for the remission of sins, and I look for the Resurrection of the dead, and the Life of the world to come. Amen.

The Apostles Creed[201] (340 AD)

I believe in God the Father Almighty, Maker of heaven and earth; And in Jesus Christ His only Son our Lord, Who was conceived by the Holy Ghost, born of the Virgin Mary, Suffered under Pontius Pilot, was crucified, dead, and buried. He descended into hell. The third day he arose from the dead. He ascended into heaven, and He sittith on the right hand of God the Father Almighty. From thence He will come to judge the quick and the dead. I believe in the Holy Ghost, the Holy Catholic Church, the Communion of Saints, the forgiveness of sins, the resurrection of the body, and the life everlasting. Amen.

---

[201] Creeds of Christendom, The. (2007). *The Creeds of Christendom With a History and Critical Notes Volume I The History of Creeds.* Baker Books. Edited by Philip Schaff. Revised by David S. Schaff. A Division of Baker Book House Company. Grand Rapids, Michigan. Pages 27-29.

The Athanasian Creed[202] (450AD)

Whosoever will be saved, before all things it is necessary that he hold the Catholic Faith: Which Faith except every one does keep whole and undefiled; without doubt he shall perish everlastingly. Of the Catholic Faith is this: That we worship one God in Trinity and Trinity in Unity; neither confounding the Persons; nor dividing the Substance (Essence). For there is one Person of the Father; another of the Son and another of the Holy Ghost. But the Godhead of the Father, of the Son, and of the Holy Ghost, is all one: the Glory equal, the Majesty coeternal. Such as the Father is: such is the Son; and such is the Holy Ghost. The Father uncreated, the Son uncreated, and the Holy Ghost uncreated. The Father incomprehensible (unlimited), the Son incomprehensible (unlimited), and the Holy Ghost incomprehensible (unlimited, or infinite). The Father eternal; the Son eternal; and the Holy Ghost eternal. And yet they are not three eternals; but one eternal. As also there are not three uncreated; nor three incomprehensible (infinite), but one uncreated; and one incomprehensible (infinite). So likewise the Father is Almighty; the Son Almighty; and the Holy Ghost Almighty. And yet they are not three Almighty's; but one Almighty. So likewise the Father is God; the Son is God; and the Holy Ghost is God. And yet they are not three Gods; but one God. So likewise the

---

[202] Creeds of Christendom, The. (2007). *The Creeds of Christendom With a History and Critical Notes Volume II The Greek and Latin Creeds with Translations.* Baker Books. Edited by Philip Schaff. Revised by David S. Schaff. A Division of Baker Book House Company. Grand Rapids, Michigan. Pages 66-71.

Father is Lord; the Son Lord; and the Holy Ghost Lord. And yet not there Lords; but one Lord. For like as we are compelled by the Christian verity; to acknowledge every Person by himself to be God and Lord: So we are forbidden by the Catholic Religion; to say, there are three Gods, or three Lords. The Father is made of none; neither created, nor begotten. The Son is of the Father alone; not made, nor created; but begotten. The Holy Ghost is of the Father and of the Son; neither made, nor created, nor begotten; but proceeding. So there is one Father, Not three Fathers; one Son, not three Sons; One Holy Ghost, not three Holy Ghosts. And in this Trinity none is a fore, or after; none is greater, or less than another (there is nothing before, or after; nothing greater or less). But the whole three Persons are coeternal, and coequal. So that is all things, as afore-said; the Unity and Trinity, and the Trinity in Unity, is to be worshiped. He therefore that will be safe must (let him) thus think of the Trinity. Furthermore it is necessary to everlasting salvation; that he also believe rightly (faithfully) the Incarnation of our Lord Jesus Christ. For the right Faith is, that we believe and confess; that our Lord Jesus Christ, the Son of God, is God and Man; God, of the Substance (Essence) of the Father; begotten before the world; and Man, of the Substance (Essence) of his Mother, born in the world. Perfect God: and Perfect Man, of a reasonable soul and human flesh subsisting. Equal to the Father, as touching his Godhead: inferior to the Father as touching his Manhood. Who although he be (is) God and Man; yet he is not too, but one Christ. One; not by conversation of the Godhead into flesh: but by taking (assumption) of the Manhood into God. One altogether; not by confusion Substance (Essence): but by Unity of Person. For as the reasonable soul and flesh is one man; so God and Man is one Christ; who suffered for our salvation: descended into hell (Hades, spirit-world): rose again the third day from the dead. He ascended into heaven, he sittith on the right hand of the Father God (God the Father) Almighty. From whence (thence) he shall come to judge the quick and the dead. At whose coming all men shall rise again with their bodies; and shall give account for their own works. And they that have done good shall go into life everlasting: and they that have done evil, into everlasting fire. This is the Catholic Faith: which accepts a man believe faithfully (truly and firmly), he cannot be saved.

In summary, our three primary creeds remind us that we believe in one God who is creator of heaven and earth. We believe that our God is also our Heavenly Father and He has one Son who is incarnate man. We believe Jesus was born of a virgin mother. We believe Jesus was crucified under Pontius Pilate. We believe Jesus descended into hell, conquered Satan and evil and was raised again in three days as it was prophesied in the Old Testament. We believe Jesus died for our sins and He is the propitiation for our sins. We believe Jesus ascended into heaven to reign with His Father and He will come again to judge all mankind. We believe in the Holy Spirit who proceeds from the Father and the Son and together they are worshipped and glorified. We believe in the universal and apostolic church. We believe in one baptism for the remission of sins and the resurrection of the dead in Christ Jesus.

As you can see the three primary creeds are an important foundation of our Christian faith and therefore play an integral part of liturgical worship. It should be noted that creeds are not limited to religious groups or denominations. Members of many social organizations, military organizations and other organizations adhere to their creeds such as the Rotary Club[203], the Kiwanis Club[204], or the Sertoma Club[205]. Therefore creeds play an important role not only in religious denominations but in the social fabric of any organization because they identify who we are and what we believe.

---

[203] Rotary Club. (2001). Random House College Dictionary. *Random House Webster's College Dictionary 2ⁿᵈ Revised and Updated Edition.* Random House, Inc. New York, New York. www.randomhouse.com. Page 1148.

[204] Kiwanis Club. (2001). Random House College Dictionary. *Random House Webster's College Dictionary 2ⁿᵈ Revised and Updated Edition.* Random House, Inc. New York, New York. www.randomhouse.com. Page 733.

[205] Sertoma Club. (2009). Encyclopedia Britannica. *Encyclopedia Britannica 2009 Deluxe Edition.* Chicago: Encyclopedia Britannica.

Chapter Nineteen

The Lord's Prayer and King David's Prayer

In the *Catechism of the Catholic Church* we read a quote from St. Thevre...se of Lisieux in her book *Manuscripts Autobiographiques*, "What is Prayer? For me prayer is a surge of the heart; it is a simple look turned toward heaven, it is a cry of recognition and of love, embracing both trial and joy".[206] Jesus Christ opens the sixth chapter in St. Matthew telling His disciples how to behave when helping the poor and needy. He does so by telling them that they should "...not let your left hand know what your right hand is doing, so that your giving may be done in secret. And your Father, who sees in secret, will reward you".[207] Jesus often prayed in private. He instructs us to pray when we can in private so that we avoid any appearance of hypocrisy. Prayer may come in many forms and can happen in many places. We can pray in church, in our vehicles on the way to work (not closing our eyes, of course), or at home. Some people think prayer is difficult. Well, it does not have to be. Prayer

---

[206] Catechism of the Catholic Church. (1995) *Second Edition Catechism of the Catholic Church Revised in Accordance with The Official Latin Text Promulgated By Pope John Paul II*. Published by Doubleday. A Division of Random House, Inc. New York, New York. Page 673.

[207] MacArthur Study Bible, The. (2010). The MacArthur Study Bible. *The MacArthur Study Bible English Standard Version*. Crossway. A publishing ministry of Good News Publishers. Wheaton, Illinois. www.esv.org. The New Testament. St. Matthew. The Gospel of Matthew 6:3-4. Page 1369.

is simply talking to God. If we can carry on a conversation with a clerk, a teacher, a policeman, or a stranger—then we should be able to speak to God. He wants us to talk to Him. Certainly, He wants us to say what is on our hearts and on our minds even though He already knows.[208] He wants to hear us say what we need to say. So we can talk to God anywhere and you may be surprised we can pray with our eyes open. And prayers do not have to be magnificent or perfect or emotional although they can be that if need be. They can be simple and to the point. One example of prayer is when my wife and I pray before meals. A friend once asked me "why don't we pray after meals"? Now, this is an interesting thought, isn't it? We do so openly and not in private which becomes an exception unless one considers that just the two of us are in private. If we are in public, we will pray over our meals quietly asking God to bless the bounty so that it will enrich and sustain us. We do this to avoid a problem in public prayer where there is an inclination as the one praying to demonstrate their personal piety. If one's motive is to bring honor to themselves as helping the poor and needy, for example, then the one praying is doing so for the wrong reasons. God will not reward a prayer given for a selfish act. In fact, you will receive no reward for your prayer and it is unlikely whether it will be answered.[209] God will reward a prayer that is given for selfless reasons.

There are several points that need to be made concerning the Lord's Prayer. First, the prayer includes eight petitions. The first three petitions concern God's holiness and purpose which are: 1) a Father in heaven whose name is holy, 2) who lives in a kingdom that will someday be established on earth, and 3) whose will is done in both heaven and earth. The next set of petitions concern

---

[208] MacArthur Study Bible, The. (2010). The MacArthur Study Bible. *The MacArthur Study Bible English Standard Version.* Crossway. A publishing ministry of Good News Publishers. Wheaton, Illinois. www.esv.org. The New Testament. St. Matthew. The Gospel of Matthew 6:7. Page 1369.

[209] MacArthur Study Bible, The. (2010). The MacArthur Study Bible. *The MacArthur Study Bible English Standard Version.* Crossway. A publishing ministry of Good News Publishers. Wheaton, Illinois. www.esv.org. The New Testament. St. Matthew. The Gospel of Matthew 6:6. Page 1369.

three personal requests which are: 1) for our daily bread, and 2) for our sins, and 3) the forgiveness of sins by others. The third set of petitions is that we be given strength to: 1) resist temptation, and 2) to protect and deliver us from evil. These three sets of petitions are important to God and to man. However, God's petitions take precedence over man's petitions and by doing so we give God honor and glory due His name.

As we pray, we are to do so with reverence and dignity. God calls us to find a quiet room, to close the door so when we speak, we can have interrupted prayer to Him who is unseen. God hears all our prayers and He answers them according to His will and when He is ready. God may not answer our prayers right away as we may wish, but He does answer all our prayers and He does so in our best interest at the best time. Our prayers must be sincere and heartfelt and realistic. A prayer that we may sprout wings and fly is not a realistic prayer. We need to make realistic prayers and petitions. Again, Jesus warns us not to pray as the Pharisee prays who does so out in the open for all to hear. Those who pray in this way do so for their own edification and their prayers are not sincere. Their public proclamation is all the reward they will receive. However, when we pray in our own privacy, God will reward us for our sincere and earnest prayers. And finally, be not afraid to ask God for the desires of your heart. In Psalm 37:4 we read, "delight yourself also in the Lord, And He shall give you the desires of your heart". God wants to give us our reasonable desires; even so, he already knows what our desires and needs are before we ask Him. Now reasonable desires are within the parameters of our creation. No, we cannot fly or be like superman but all other reasonable desires, He will answer. And that answer may sometimes be no because God ultimately knows what is best for us when we do not know ourselves. The purpose of praying to God is for one reason only. It demonstrates our obedience to Him and in our prayer life. So pray often and sincerely and God will answer all our prayers and don't be afraid to ask for the desires of your heart.

There are only two Gospels where the Lord's Prayer is recorded. They are the Gospels of St. Matthew and St. Luke. Jesus tells His twelve disciples in the early part of His ministry how to pray when they asked, "Lord, teach us to pray".[210] In the Gospel of Matthew we read the following:

> *"Our Father which art in heaven, hallowed be thy name. Thy kingdom come. Thy will be done in earth, as it is in heaven. Give us this day our daily bread. And forgive us our debts, as we forgive our debtors. And lead us not into temptation, but deliver us from evil: for thine is the kingdom, and the power, and the glory, forever. Amen".*[211]

Now, the Lord's Prayer ends at 'deliver us from evil' in the Roman Catholic Church. However, there is a doxology that was added by the Reformers of the Protestant movement and although it is not recorded in the original Greek text, it is recorded in the 1611 version of the King James Bible. The doxology is written as, *"For thine is the kingdom, and the power, and the glory, forever. Amen".*[212] Many Protestant churches say this prayer and where we read debts and debtors; some recite trespasses and trespass instead.

In the following paragraphs I have analyzed the passages for your deeper understanding and edification in hope that you will realize the words of Christ and what they mean. I pray they will have a positive impact on your life. They begin as follows:

Our Father which art in heaven, addresses to whom the prayer is given and establishes the personal or childlike nature of our relationship with God. It also identifies where our Father lives, on

---

[210] MacArthur Study Bible, The. (2010). The MacArthur Study Bible. *The MacArthur Study Bible English Standard Version*. Crossway. A publishing ministry of Good News Publishers. Wheaton, Illinois. www.esvbible.org. The New Testament. St. Luke. The Gospel of Luke 11:1. Page1498.

[211] Holy Bible, The. (2004). The Holy Bible. *The Holy Bible Authorized King James Version*. World Publishing. Nashville, Tennessee. www.worldpublishing.com. The New Testament. St. Matthew. The Gospel of Matthew 6:9-13. Page 423.

[212] Holy Bible, The. (2005). *The Holy Bible 1611 Edition King James Version*. Hendrickson Publishers, Inc. Peabody, Massachusetts. The New Testament. St. Matthew. The Gospel of Matthew 6:13. Page not numbered.

His throne in heaven. God is known to have walked on earth in the Garden of Eden[213] with Adam and Eve and there are many other occasions of His presence on earth as when He descended on Mt. Sinai[214] to write the Ten Commandments or when He spoke from a burning bush.[215]

Hallowed be thy name acknowledges the sovereignty of God. We petition God with reverence and dignity due His name. The name of God commands respect and awe. Our world tries to belittle the name of God when His name is blasphemed although it should invoke fear in terms of respect. God is both frightening and wonderful in the same utterance. I am sure He is frightening for those who do not know Him.

Thy kingdom come is a reference to the coming of Christ's kingdom on earth. The second coming (Christ's first coming was His birth in the manger in Bethlehem, Judea) as well as His first was predicted by the prophets of the Old Testament. He proclaims His second coming in the gospels and His second coming is described in more detail in Revelation and it will be precipitated by the evil in the world being destroyed. The world will not end except for the evil and the new kingdom on earth will be ruled by Christ the bridegroom and His bride[216] the church.

Thy will be done in earth, as it is in heaven follows the sovereignty of God along with the praise and worship of God. God is our creator and He will bring His kingdom on earth and we will

---

[213] Holy Bible, The. (2004). The Holy Bible. *The Holy Bible Authorized King James Version.* World Publishing. Nashville, Tennessee. www.worldpublishing.com. The Old Testament. Moses. The Book of Genesis 2:8. Page 9.

[214] Holy Bible, The. (2004). The Holy Bible. *The Holy Bible Authorized King James Version.* World Publishing. Nashville, Tennessee. www.worldpublishing.com. The Old Testament. Moses. The Book of Exodus 19:18. Page 109.

[215] Believer's Study Bible, The. (1991). The Believer's Study Bible. *The Believer's Study Bible New King James Version.* Thomas Nelson Publishers. Nashville, Tennessee. The Old Testament. Moses. The Book of Exodus 3:6. Page 83; The New Testament. St. Mark. The Gospel of Mark 12:36. Page 1419.

[216] Holy Bible, The. (2004). The Holy Bible. *The Holy Bible Authorized King James Version.* World Publishing. Nashville, Tennessee. www.worldpublishing.com. The New Testament. St. John. The Book of Revelation 19:7. Page 550.

share in that kingdom. By praying for God's kingdom on earth, we are asking His will be done in our lives for His kingdom will come when His will is fulfilled. Our reward is the kingdom of God and it is reserved for those who do the will of God and we will share in that kingdom as sons of God.

Give us this day our daily bread means both food for our bodies and food for our souls. Jesus tells us that a man does not live by bread alone[217]. We need sustenance in the form of bread or manna both for our physical bodies as well as sustenance in the form of God's Word for our spiritual bodies. Two of Christ's miracles were the feeding of the five thousand[218] on the mount and four thousand[219] on the plain. In both cases Christ fed the thousands with the manna of bread and fish. Then He fed His disciples and their followers with the bread of life, God's Word.

And forgive us our debts, as we forgive our debtors means just what it says. When we ask God to forgive us of our sins, we are obligated to forgive those who sinned against us. This is the penitential portion of the Lord's Prayer. This point is critical for the Scriptures teach us that if we cannot forgive those who sin against us then we cannot expect God to forgive us our sins. We must have a spirit of forgiveness in our hearts and live righteously. When we receive the gift of forgiveness from God, then we are to share that spirit of forgiveness with each other. When we do forgive others, they receive a gift from God. When we accept Jesus Christ as our Lord and Savior, we accept certain obligations as members of God's family and it is pertinent to how we treat each other both believers and unbelievers. Believers are to forgive each other as God does for Christ's sake who was the propitiation of

---

[217] Holy Bible, The. (2004). The Holy Bible. *The Holy Bible Authorized King James Version.* World Publishing. Nashville, Tennessee. www.worldpublishing.com. The New Testament. St. Luke. The Gospel of Luke 4:4. Page 451.

[218] Holy Bible, The. (2004). The Holy Bible. *The Holy Bible Authorized King James Version.* World Publishing. Nashville, Tennessee. www.worldpublishing.com. The New Testament. St. Matthew. The Gospel of Matthew 14:21. Page 428.

[219] Holy Bible, The. (2004). The Holy Bible. *The Holy Bible Authorized King James Version.* World Publishing. Nashville, Tennessee. www.worldpublishing.com. The New Testament. St. Matthew. The Gospel of Matthew 15:38. Page 429.

our sins and paid the price for our sins with His blood[220]. If we choose not to forgive others, then we jeopardize God's forgiveness of our sins.[221] Another version calls for the forgiveness for sins and debts of omission and commission. In other words, we are asking forgiveness for sins we commit that are known and sins that we commit that are unknown.

And lead us not into temptation is where we ask for God's continued presence with us as we live in this world to protect us from the evil that stalks us. God promises us in the Scriptures that He will not allow us to meet any temptation that He does not leave us a way to escape. He also promises us that we will never experience a temptation that we will not be able to resist on our own or with His help. St. Paul tells us that the flesh wars with our spirit so we are tempted daily[222]. We pray then that God will aid us in our struggles with temptation and with Satan and his army[223]. By praying to God for guidance we seek God's will in our lives and not Satan's will.

But deliver us from evil has two meanings. We are asking for deliverance from our sins as well as deliverance from the devil and his legions.

For thine is the kingdom, and the power, and the glory, forever. Amen is a doxology that was added by Protestant reformers in the 1611 Holy Bible, King James Version. This doxology was written

---

[220] Believer's Study Bible, The. (1991). The Believer's Study Bible. *The Believer's Study Bible New King James Version.* Thomas Nelson Publishers. Nashville, Tennessee. The New Testament. St. Paul. The Letter of Paul to the Ephesians 4:32. Page 1681.

[221] Believer's Study Bible, The. (1991). The Believer's Study Bible. *The Believer's Study Bible New King James Version.* Thomas Nelson Publishers. Nashville, Tennessee. The New Testament. St. Paul. The Letter of Paul to the Colossians' 3:13. Page 1699.

[222] Believer's Study Bible, The. (1991). The Believer's Study Bible. *The Believer's Study Bible New King James Version.* Thomas Nelson Publishers. Nashville, Tennessee. The New Testament. St. Paul. The Letter of Paul to the Galatians 5:17. Page 1672.

[223] Believer's Study Bible, The. (1991). The Believer's Study Bible. *The Believer's Study Bible New King James Version.* Thomas Nelson Publishers. Nashville, Tennessee. The New Testament. St. Paul. The Letter of Paul to the Ephesians 6:12. Page 1683.

in the Stephen's version of the Greek New Testament as well as the Didache[224] which is a compilation of lessons given to the earliest Gentile Christians by some of the original Apostles. This early doxology could very well be the basis of the reformers doxology. Eastern Orthodox Church and Eastern Catholic Church priests sing during the Divine Service, the following doxology, 'for thine is the kingdom and the power and the glory, of the Father, and of the Son, and of the Holy Spirit, now and forever and unto the ages of ages'. However, the doxology is not recited in either the Roman Catholic Church's Roman Rite Mass as well as some Lutheran Churches including the Missouri Church Lutheran Synod. The Roman Catholics end the Lord's Prayer at 'but deliver us from evil'. Finally, a similar doxology is found in the in the Old Testament where we read a prayer by King David. His prayer in chapter twenty-nine of the first Book of Chronicles and the Lord's Prayer in St. Matthew chapter six, and St. Luke chapter eleven are not often compared to each other but I thought the reader would enjoy this short exercise. In the first Book of Chronicles, King David offers a prayer as follows:

> '...Praise be to you, O Lord, God of our Father Israel, from everlasting to everlasting. Yours, O Lord, is the greatness and the power and the glory and the majesty and the splendor, for everything in heaven and earth is yours. Yours, O Lord, is the kingdom; you are exalted as head over all. Wealth and honor come from you; you are the ruler of all things. In your hands are strength and power to exalt and give strength to all. Now, our God, we give you thanks, and praise your glorious name'.[225]

---

[224] Didache, The. (2010). *The Didache A Window on the Earliest Christians.* SPCK. Baker Academic. A Division of Baker Publishing Group. www.bakeracademic.com. Grand Rapids, Michigan. Thomas O'Loughlin, Editor. Page 166.

[225] Believer's Study Bible, The. (1991). The Believer's Study Bible. *The Believer's Study Bible New King James Version.* Thomas Nelson Publishers. Nashville, Tennessee. The Old Testament. The first Book of Chronicles 29:10-15. Pages 585-586.

As you can see, some of the components of King David's prayer are similar to the Lord's Prayer. They both begin with the same reverence, worship and praise. They speak of God's kingdom in both heaven and earth. And they have similar doxologies. I do not believe that it is a coincidence that King David's prayer and the Lord's Prayer are similar. I believe the person of Jesus Christ has the same knowledge as God His Father. Jesus is a descendent of King David, the king God says, is 'a man after my own heart'.[226] David the political leader and King of the Jews represents the Old Covenant with God and Israel; while the spiritual leader Jesus, the King of the Jews, represents the New Covenant with all the people including the Jews and the Gentiles.

King David's Prayer is given to an eternal God without beginning or ending. This is a fundamental understanding of God. David worships and praises God with due reverence, fear and awe. This type of attitude opens a dialogue with God because it shows God that King David (and us if we incorporate this kind of disposition in our prayer) knows who He is; a God who commands respect. Incidentally, this is why, when we enter a sanctuary, we are to be respectful and reverent. It is not a social hour like many 'worshippers' have made it. Once praise is established like it is in the Lord's Prayer, then petitions to our Heavenly Father may be added. All these conditions present a heart of worship where the body and mind and soul, or our metaphysical nature are in unison focusing solely on God's glory, laud, and honor. David's Prayer is made on behalf of Israel and it is centered on the belief that all things in heaven and on earth are owned by God because He created it. Anything that we have in our possession is because God allows us to share it with Him. When we die, we return to ashes and dust and nothing we have gained or acquired on this earth will be taken with us into eternity although many including the Pharaoh's of Egypt have tried. In eternity, God will provide for us, clothe us, feed us, and house us. Beyond food, clothing, and housing, there

---

[226] Holy Bible, The. (2004). The Holy Bible. *The Holy Bible Authorized King James Version*. World Publishing. Nashville, Tennessee. www.worldpublishing.com. The New Testament. The Acts of the Apostles. St. Luke. Luke 13:22. Page 488.

is nothing else we need except God. King David knew how to pray to God as much as Christ Jesus knew how to pray to God, His Father. If one considers the Psalms as prayers, which they are, then King David had more recorded prayers in the Bible than anyone else. Perhaps no one knew the importance of prayer, outside of His Son Jesus, more than King David. From the commandments to the creeds and now learning how to communicate with God, if you incorporate these principles in your daily life you will begin to live a life on the precepts of sacred theism.

Chapter Twenty

The Seven Holy Sacraments or Mysteries

There are seven Holy Sacraments or Holy Mysteries. Two are major sacraments and five are minor sacraments (called mysteries in the Orthodox Church). The description of major or minor is questionable since all should be treated with equal reverence. One reason that only two sacraments are called major is because they are the only ones explicitly ordained by Christ. The two major sacraments are Holy Communion (Holy Eucharist) and Holy Baptism. The five minor sacraments are implied in the New Testament.

Since the Protestant Reformation, the two major sacraments of Communion and Baptism are readily accepted by most denominations. However, the five minor sacraments of Holy Orders, Holy Confirmation, Holy Matrimony, Extreme Unction and Penance are by and large not adhered except for Holy Matrimony by most Protestant Churches. Ironically the lackadaisical treatment of the five minor sacraments has affected the two major sacraments since the two major sacraments are being practiced fewer times than they were in the past. There is a strong indication, although not scientific, that the two major sacraments of Holy Communion and Holy Baptism are becoming less important to the average worshiper. In fact, at a recent convention of a major denomination, an amendment to the canons was submitted to allow those not baptized to participate in Holy Communion. Participation in Holy Communion is one of the benefits of being a member of the body of Christ. In the Thirty-Nine Articles of Religion we read that participation in communion without baptism or membership in Christ's church is essentially a cardinal sin. Fortunately this measure failed but the proponents will surely bring it up again in the future. It is as if today's church leadership is blind to the truth of Scripture and does not understand the church doctrine and merits of the canons and why they have been institutionalized for hundreds of years.

Many Protestant churches (with the exception of many liturgical churches who celebrate most every Sunday) had a practice of celebrating Holy Communion at least once a month. The regular occurrence in many Protestant churches has been reduced to once every quarter. This quarterly practice is being reduced even further to perhaps twice a year. One would think if the trend continues that the participation in Holy Communion will soon be a thing of the past. This point can be underscored in Gregg R. Allison's book, *Historical Theology,*[227] where he points out the view of Baptists, after this denomination's founder, John Smyth, declared that "the Lord's Supper is the external sign of the communion with Christ". His fellow Baptist believer Thomas Helwys further added that the "observance should be (a) part of every worship service, the Lord's Supper should be administered every Sunday...(the) Baptists soon switched to monthly administration out of concern that frequent celebrations would result in a sacramental ritualism similar to that of the (Roman) Catholic Mass, and for fear that frequent observation of the Lord's Supper would detract from the central element of preaching the Word of God". This clearly shows a distinction between traditional liturgical churches (Anglican, Roman, and Orthodox) who regularly observe Holy Communion and their reformed Protestant siblings. As far as the sacrament of Holy Baptism is concerned, its regularity is dependent on new

---

[227] Historical Theology. (2011). *A Companion to Wayne Grudem's Systematic Theology Historical Theology An Introduction to Christian Doctrine.* Zondervan. Grand Rapids, Michigan. Gregg R. Allison. Page 656.

converts; and in the case of Holy Matrimony, is dependent on when nuptials decide to marry.

Traditional liturgical denominations regularly observe worship services containing both the Word and the sacrament. Many Protestant churches observe worship services by proclaiming the Word and omitting the sacrament. It seems these Protestant churches do not put as high a premium on the observance of sacraments as do the traditional liturgical churches. Starting with the Protestant Reformation and subsequently thereafter, the reformers changed the service of Word and sacrament and settled on the Word-only service. Traditional symbols were also discarded in many Protestant churches with a few exceptions. The five additional sacraments were largely dismissed by the reformers and never regularly observed except for Holy Matrimony.

Again, as I mentioned in an earlier chapter, a traditional liturgical church will include a center aisle called Jacobs Ladder that leads up to the altar which increasingly elevates. This is a symbol of hiking up to the cross and climbing the ladder to heaven. Ironically, many Protestant church aisles descend to the pulpit rather than ascend. I hope this design is not symbolic and hopefully it lacks symbolism altogether. We should be headed up to heaven and not the other way around. In the liturgical setting, the focus is on the cross and Christ Jesus, not as viewed in the Protestant churches where the focus is on the pulpit and the pastor. Even the choirs in the liturgical churches face the altar or each other from the chancel while Protestant choirs face the congregation. They appear to bear down on the pulpit where the Word is proclaimed. Many traditional liturgical churches architecture is designed in the form of a cross. In contrast, many Protestant churches architecture is designed on a circular fashion. I mentioned these symbols again to remind the reader that as Christians we have many approaches in our forms of worship. Liturgical symbols, traditions, customs, and practices all combine to create an atmosphere that is conducive to the highest forms of worship. Emphasis is either on the Word or on the combined Word and sacrament. This is a monumental distinction and it affects how we view worship.

Let us review the meaning of a sacrament.[228] A sacrament is the 'outward and visible sign of an inward and spiritual grace'. The sacrament of Holy Communion is referenced by the Last Supper in the Gospels of Matthew 26:17; Mark 14:12; and Luke 22:7. In this sacrament the outward and visible sign is the bread and wine while the inward and spiritual grace is the grace received. Reference to this grace is found on page 82 of the 1928 *Book of Common Prayer* where we read, "Grant us therefore, gracious Lord, so to eat the flesh of thy Son Jesus Christ, and to drink his blood, that our sinful bodies may be made clean by His body, and our souls washed through His most precious blood, and that we may evermore dwell in Him, and He in us". This Scripture does not mean the actual flesh and blood of Christ, but it means with the Real Presence of Jesus Christ. In other words, He is with us in Spirit. When we consume the consecrated bread and wine representing Jesus Christ, and as it is digested, it becomes a part of us in our blood and flesh. Therefore, we are in Him and He is in us. In the sacrament of *Holy Baptism* which is mentioned again in the Gospels of Matthew 3:13; Mark 1:9; and Luke 3:21, the outward and visible sign is the water while the inward and spiritual grace given is the indwelling of the Holy Spirit. It is important to note that some denominations believe in multiple baptisms. This is apostasy and heresy all wrapped into one. Once baptized, always baptized. Baptism is a rebirth. Just as we are born once physically from our mother's womb, we are born once spiritually in Holy Baptism. As the Scripture says, we cannot reenter our mother's womb to be reborn; even so we cannot be reborn in Holy Baptism.

As for the lesser five sacraments that are alluded in *Holy Matrimony*, there are numerous examples of marriage between one man and one woman in both the Old and New Testaments, not the least of which is in the book of Genesis between Adam and Eve. The outward and visible sign is the wedding ring and the inward and spiritual grace is the union in-one. The next sacrament,

---

[228] Sacrament. (2010). *Christianity The First Three Thousand Years.* Viking. Published by the Penguin Group. Penguin Group (USA), Inc. New York, New York. Diarmaid MacCulloch. Pages 620-622.

in no particular order, is *Holy Orders* which is the ordination of clergy. We read about clergy in the Old Testament and the New Testament being sustained through the unbroken line of Apostolic Succession.[229] The references are found in the books of Exodus 29:9; Leviticus 8:1; and Hebrews 7:11. The outward and visible sign of Holy Orders is the laying on of hands, the applying of holy oil and the binding of hands by the ordaining bishop, and the inward and spiritual grace is the grace received. This grace is passed down from Jesus Christ through the Apostles who were given power to administer the sacraments of the Church. Just like the tribe of Levi who God called to be the priests of the Israel in the Old Testament; they were the only ones allowed to conduct worship services, enter the sacristy or holy of holies or to administer sacrifices. Now, a new order of priests was established under Christ and they follow in the Apostolic Order as ordained to administer the sacraments and proclaim the Word of God. This is the Holy Order of the Church and it is the grace given through Apostolic Succession from Jesus Christ. The symbol of this priestly order is the white collar worn by priests of the liturgical background. Those who are not of the liturgical background or apostolic succession should not be wearing the collar because it is not a symbol of all ministers as some would have you believe. If ministers want to wear the collar, then they must submit to the episcopal oversight of a bishop and adhere to the canons that regulate liturgical priests.

The sacrament of *Holy Confirmation* is found in several verses of the Old and New Testaments including the books of Exodus 26:1; Psalm 109:106; and Acts 14:3. The outward and visible sign is the laying hands on the head of the confirmand by the bishop and the inward and spiritual grace is being received as a member in the family of God and Christ's kingdom. In the sacrament of *Holy Penance*, again there are several references in Scripture in both the Old and New Testaments which include the books of Leviticus 5:16; Proverbs 27:12; and Romans 1:27. The outward and

---

[229] Apostolic Succession. (2010) *Christianity The First Three Thousand Years.* Viking. Published by the Penguin Group. Penguin Group (USA), Inc. New York, New York. Diarmaid MacCulloch. Pages 620-622.

visible sign is punishment and the inward and spiritual grace is the redeeming grace of our sins being forgiven. And finally the sacrament of *Extreme Unction* is found in numerous verses in both testaments including verses in the books of Exodus 29:7; Leviticus 14:18; and Matthew 6:17. The outward and visible sign is the holy oil and the inward and spiritual grace is the healing or cleansing.

The counterparts to the seven Great Mysteries in the Orthodox Christian church are Holy Communion, Holy Baptism, Ordination (Holy Orders), Chrismation (Confirmation), Confession (Penance), Unction (Extreme Unction), and Holy Matrimony. The importance here is that the liturgical traditions continue to be observed when necessary in the seven sacraments (mysteries) unlike the nonliturgical churches.

As a special note, Anglicans are not in full communion with the Roman Church so there is no Anglican Christian who can receive Holy Eucharist at a Roman Church. Many church leaders in the Roman Catholic Church still believe that the Anglican Communion is of an invalid order making the participation in Holy Eucharist invalid.

Roman Catholic visitors at an Anglican Church typically do not participate in Holy Eucharist although they are welcomed if they are baptized Christians. Until the validity of Holy Orders is recognized by both communions, there is still a stretch of road to travel in order to share in Holy Eucharist at either church. This is not limited solely to the Holy Eucharist. In Holy Orders, a priest cannot celebrate or conduct services in a church wherein he is not licensed. And as far as Holy Baptism, most liturgical churches baptize or christen at an early age. Many Protestant denominations wait until the age of twelve or the age of accountability.

Therefore, once again, as you develop a life in practice of sacred theism, after learning the creeds, the Decalogue and the Summary of the Law, and how to pray; the next logical step is to participate in the holy sacraments or mysteries. This will afford the Christian all the steps necessary to live a life of joy and gladness in the study and worship of our one God who created us all. Then we will become wired to Him.

Chapter Twenty One

The Articles of Religion

Generally, the Anglican *Articles of Religion* is an expanded creed as well as the Westminster Confession[230], the Catechism of the Catholic Church, the Augsburg Confession[231], the Creeds of the Orthodox Church[232] as well as the numerous other creeds, confessions or articles. All creeds can be expounded upon and this section could have easily been included in chapter eighteen on the *Three Primary Creeds*. However, I decided to write a chapter on the Anglican Communion's *Thirty-Nine Articles of Religion* because it is largely a summary of all the creeds and principles of every Christian denomination.

This chapter is the last of five segments in Part Two and represents why the term pentagon was used. It represents a

---

[230] Westminster Confession. (2007). The Creeds of Christendom. *The Creeds of Christendom With a History and Critical Notes Volume I The History of Creeds*. Baker Books. Edited by Philip Schaff. Revised by David S. Schaff. A Division of Baker Book House Company. Grand Rapids, Michigan. Pages 753-782.

[231] Augsburg Confession. (2007). The Creeds of Christendom. *The Creeds of Christendom With a History and Critical Notes Volume I History of Creeds*. Baker Books. Edited by Philip Schaff. Revised by David S. Schaff. A Division of Baker Book House Company. Grand Rapids, Michigan. Pages 225-246.

[232] Creeds of the Greek Church, The. (2007). The Creeds of Christendom. *The Creeds of Christendom With a History and Critical Notes Volume I The History of Creeds*. Baker Books. Edited by Philip Schaff. Revised By David S. Schaff. A Division of Baker Book House Company. Grand Rapids, Michigan. Pages 43-78.

five corner design as well as the military building in Arlington, Virginia which is a symbol of the United States Military. It causes us to think in military terms because we are in a spiritual battle for our very souls and the souls of millions of people. The lessons you learn in this book, *The Pentagon of Faith: Sacred Theism vs. Secular Humanism A Christian's Need for the Traditional Faith of Our Fathers*, will help restore you to a Godly life of sacred theism and give you the ammunition to defend yourself in the battle against the evil of secular humanism. References to secular humanism were taken from many articles and books including the internet because it is a term developed and understood over the past fifty years. The idiom sacred theism is altogether new so references to this term were largely taken from the Holy Scriptures.

Now you may say that I favor the Thirty-Nine Articles of Religion and perhaps I do since I am an Anglican, but in fairness, these thirty-nine articles do represent the highest percentage of all the rules and definitions that comprise the Christian faith. The thirty-nine articles did not become what they represent overnight. Indeed, they began as thirteen articles in 1538, then forty-two articles in 1553 and finally thirty-nine articles in 1571. So over the course of thirty three years, a consensus was reached to summarize the core beliefs of Christianity. They represent the clarity of Christian doctrine that includes the best from both sides of the reformed Protestants and traditional Catholic bodies. They were extensively debated by the most thoughtful and educated minds of their time around the world when they were conceived and written over five hundred years ago.

I know that some of my brothers and sisters in the Orthodox and Roman communions may question some of the statements in this segment, largely because the Articles of Religion were written by Anglican scholars, but I ask their indulgence and hope they give credit to the premise. The Articles of Religion are estimated as representing better than ninety-five percent of the agreed upon beliefs of every Christian. There are only a few basic doctrines, although these may be no more than educated opinions, which separate us where perhaps a better understanding could bridge the gap. The Articles of Religion are offered here because they summarize more clearly the essence of our beliefs for the unfamiliar reader or unbeliever who is curious of the Christian tradition. Personally, I would rather see Christianity united than divided. We have already been splintered enough. The fine tuning has already been debated by theological titans over the centuries. Suffice it to say that the Christian Church split at the one thousand year mark over theology, and again five hundred years later during the Protestant Reformation. These two major mile-stones or schisms were more than a split; they were more like the tweaking of the truth of the Holy Scriptures. I do not mean to make light of the issues in the debates at the time, but for whatever reasons the scholars and clergy reached an impasse. These schisms caused the opposing sides to go their separate ways. Therefore, what I am contending in this book, in the light of the Summary of the Law, that modern Christian theology has been tweaked over fifteen hundred years and there are scarce reasons to tweak it anymore. Further tweaking could place us upon the threshold of another schism and perhaps venturing into apostasy and we are seeing hints of that today. There have already been disruptions in the churches with respect to homosexual ordination into Holy Orders and the movement of radical sexism intervening to change the sex of God and make marriage between same-sex individuals canon law. These tweaks can be considered symptoms of an overall contempt for the authority of the Holy Scriptures.

    Let's look at one of the fundamental reasons for this book. It is written to provide Christians a reference to the Holy Scripture as well as other theological writings that can explain why we call ourselves Christians. We have somehow failed to understand who we are, and what and why we believe. This book can help Christians focus on these questions and help us to take a stand for the truth of the Gospel in order to prevent further theological apostasy when it arises as we have seen over the course of time. And no, we do not need to merge Christianity with other world religions as the current forces of secular humanism wish. Perhaps

I should have written more about this trend but I chose to focus on the individual Christian with hopes they will grow into an army of true believers. However, there is an active movement to combine the world's religions into one religion. This is absurd and God will not stand for it. A one world religion as promoted by the forces of secular humanism is not realistic but it could happen according to the Scriptures. There is already a movement to combine Christianity and Islam into one religion called Chrislam. If the innocent followers knew what a mistake this would be, then my hope is that they would turn away from this radical idea. Here again is a necessary reason for *The Pentagon of Faith*. Consider in chapter one where we read how I could have easily been misled in the debate I had with the Muslim man if it were not for my knowledge of the entire truth of the Holy Scriptures. Many so-called Christians would have fallen for this trap because they are scripturally and spiritually weak. Again, *The Pentagon of Faith* is intended to help fill the void by including the five segments on core Christian beliefs in Part Two.

I have always tried to stay above the fray unless the theology was blatant apostasy. I have made a point to fulfill the law as Christ has taught us in the Summary of the Law. We are to love the Lord our God with all our heart, all our soul, and all our mind and the second is like unto it to love our neighbor as ourselves. Remember, this passage ends with the statement that on these two commandments hang all the law and the prophets. To me this ends the debate. However, if we focus on the *Summary of the Law*, our differences become largely a matter of semantics. For instance, if we Anglicans and Orthodox Christians delve into the debate over consubstantiation[233] versus transubstantiation[234] with our Roman

---

[233] Consubstantiation. (2011). Historical Theology. *A Companion to Wayne Grudem's Systematic Theology Historical Theology An Introduction to Christian Doctrine.* Zondervan. Grand Rapids, Michigan. Gregg R. Allison. Pages 657-658.

[234] Transubstantiation.(1995). Catechism of the Catholic Church. *Second Edition Catechism of the Catholic Church Revised in Accordance with The Official Latin Text Promulgated By Pope John Paul II.* Published by Doubleday. A Division of Random House, Inc. New York, New York. Pages 1373-1377.

siblings are we less faithful if we choose one over the other? Have we not ultimately fulfilled the command by Christ to, 'do this in remembrance of me.'[235] Or if we Anglican and Roman Catholics debate our Orthodox siblings over the reference of sacraments as mysteries, are we lessening the validity of the outward and visible sign of an inward and spiritual grace?

I am a traditionalist but in light of church attendance declining and the figures are alarming, should we as Christian leadership not be encouraged when new people are at least attending services and worshipping our Heavenly Father? I mean, if we get close enough to the fire, maybe our hardened hearts and minds will melt away and open us to the truth inherent in God's Word. Maybe we can encourage our progressive Protestant siblings to incorporate more liturgical practice into their worship services by including more sacramental observation in association with the preached Word.

In the catholic tradition, and I do not mean Roman, the customs and rituals are implied in the traditional faith of our church fathers. Arguments opposing traditional worship are made routinely. There is a common saying that 'all roads lead to the Cross at Calvary'. However, I would caution everyone to remember that there is still only one way to heaven and that is through Jesus Christ who says in John 14:6, "I am the Way and the Truth and the Life. No one comes to the Father except through Me". I do not pretend that everyone is persuaded by the same forces. Indeed, some people are moved by their emotions while others are led by their intellect. People from all walks of life and levels of abilities become believers of Christ Jesus. A Christian has many stripes like the zebra and God made everyone unique. I wrote a sermon once that quoted B.H. Streeter[236] who argues that worship is largely

---

[235] Holy Bible, The. (2004). The Holy Bible. *The Holy Bible Authorized King James Version.* World Publishing. Nashville, Tennessee. www.worldpublishing.com. The New Testament. St. Paul. The first Letter of Paul to the Corinthians 11:25. Page 509.

[236] Primitive Church, The. (1929). *The Primitive Church.* Author B.H. Streeter. The MacMillan Company. New York, New York. Page 268.

a matter of the individual. He wrote, '*the greatest obstacle (to Union) is the belief...that there is some one form of Church Order which alone is primitive, and which, therefore, alone possesses the sanction of Apostolic precedent...In the Primitive Church no one system of Church order prevailed. Everywhere there was readiness to experiment, and where circumstances seemed to demand it, to change...It may be that the line of advance for the Church of today is not to imitate the forms, but to recapture the spirit of the Primitive Church.*'

The first part of his argument is somewhat flawed because the primitive church was in its infancy and in the initial process of developing a tradition and liturgical form of worship. Obviously, there was no traditional or unified order of worship in the early days when it was just then being developed by the Apostles and early Christians. And the manner of worship was corporate in its development. If we recapture the spirit as he says, then we need to return to the traditional faith of our fathers and I might add their traditional ways of worship.

The doctrine of the Apostolic Succession is gleaned from Scripture and is supported by the early church fathers. It is a doctrine of apostolic succession wherein Jesus Christ gave the sacramental authority of the Church in Holy Orders making bishops of the Apostles. They, in turn, gave full sacramental orders to their successors. Therefore, today's bishops, priests and deacons can trace their succession to the Twelve Apostles and Jesus Christ. However, this is a different story in the Protestant denominations (Anglican Church excluded). Most Protestant clergy do not recognize the apostolic succession because they cannot trace their succession which makes their Holy Orders invalid. They claim that the gifts given by Christ to His Apostles cannot be passed to the next generation. If this argument were true then, we cannot pass our DNA from one generation to the next. Therefore, Protestant clergy view the apostolic succession as a faithful succession of Christ's teachings.

Many Protestant clergy disagree with the Doctrine of Apostolic Succession as in the case of Norman L. Geisler who in his book Systematic Theology[237] claimed that the gifts of the Apostles ended in the first century when they died. Well, of course he would take this position because he was not from the universal catholic tradition and was not a beneficiary of the succession. Is it necessary to deny a two thousand year tradition when we need to focus on unity to fight the forces of secular humanism and practice the elements of the Summary of the Law? Can we not put our petty differences aside and worship as one body of Christians?

Again, in reference to Streeter's writing, he claims a need to 'recapture the spirit of the primitive church' and tradition where the primitive church ultimately developed as a mature church body. In the Interpreter's Bible, Streeter's writing is summarized in the following, 'there is no one type of service which all Christian people ought to see to be the Christian type, and so seeing, adopt and practice it. Men are built upon different lines. For some, grandeur and ceremony, even a measure of pomp are required if they are to feel themselves in the presence of God and be able really to worship him. But others draw far closer to him through the medium of the simplest of services, with nothing in it to catch and hold and, as these folk feel, distract the mind and eyes. To endeavor to contort the one or the other into the opposite, and for them, unnatural, type is futile. And indeed, why should it be attempted? There is one flock, and one shepherd. There is on Lord, one faith, one baptism.[238] There is one army of the living God. But an army may have many regiments. And it is questionable if that army would be more efficient if they, with their honors and traditions, were obliterated in one unbroken and mechanical

---

[237] Apostolic Succession. (2011). Systematic Theology in One Volume. *Systematic Theology in One Volume Bible God Creation Sin Salvation Church Last Times.* Bethany House. Minneapolis, Minnesota. Norman L. Geisler. Pages 1125-1126.

[238] Holy Bible, The. (2004). The Holy Bible. *The Holy Bible Authorized King James Version.* World Publishing. Nashville, Tennessee. www.worldpublishing.com. St. Paul. The Letter of Paul to the Galatians 4:5. Page 519.

unity."[239] Here, Streeter makes a good argument but it is flawed because in hindsight we can attribute, at least in part, the dilution of church worship and the falling away of the faithful to the era of non-liturgical worship.

Certainly we are all unique in our providential design and makeup. God created us with our own fingerprint and knows the number of the hairs on our heads. Our physical bodies have many parts each with their own unique functions. If we compare our physical bodies to the body of the Church, then we find many parts and many different functions of worship and practice. Generally, these forms of worship can be indexed or categorized into two areas of practice and worship such as contemporary and liturgical. Each person has to find the type of worship that meets their spiritual needs. However, as we find that place where we commune with God, there are some areas that are not negotiable. As we read in the wedding feast in the Gospel of St. Matthew, the host invited all into the banquet, as long as they were clothed in repentance and righteousness and these are the areas we cannot change or modify *"for many are called and few are chosen."*[240] Therefore we cannot separate the preaching and teaching of the word and the celebration of the sacrament in our worship services.

There is a time and a season for all things and Sunday worship is not the same as going to a game or attending a rock and roll concert. I am contending that we have taken our unique brand of independence too far as individuals. In the book of Ecclesiastes we read, *'there is a time for everything and a season for every activity under heaven; a time to be born and a time to die, a time to plant and a time to uproot, a time to kill and a time to heal, a time to tear down and a time to build, a time to weep and a time to laugh,*

---

[239] Interpreters Bible, The. (1952). The Interpreter's Bible. *The Interpreter's Bible The Holy Scriptures in the King James and Revised Standard Versions with General Articles and Introduction, Exegesis, Exposition for Each Book of the Bible In Twelve Volumes Volume VIII The Gospel According to St. Luke The Gospel According to St. John.* Abington Press. Nashville, Tennessee. Page 627.

[240] Holy Bible, The. (2004). The Holy Bible. *The Holy Bible Authorized King James Version.* World Publishing. Nashville, Tennessee. www.worldpublishing.com. St.

a time to mourn and a time to dance, a time to scatter stones and a time to gather them, a time to embrace and a time to refrain, a time to search and a time to give up, a time to keep and a time to throw away, a time to tear and a time to mend, a time to be silent and a time to speak, a time to love and a time to hate, a time for war and a time for peace.'[241] According to the Decalogue, Sunday is a day to keep holy and worship is a time for reverence and respect with dignity in which we are to worship one God, not ourselves. Dignity and respect is shown by the way we dress and the way we conduct ourselves. We should be on our best behavior because we are in the church in the presence of God, in the holy of holies. I might add that the time before worship service is not a social hour. We should spend the few minutes before worship service meditating and getting our minds and hearts ready to hear the Word and receive the sacrament of Holy Communion.

This is one of the reasons the *Thirty-nine Articles of Religion* are so important. We bear witness here to one of the main problems between non-liturgical and liturgical churches' contrasting forms of the worship service. I had a long and mentally illuminating discussion with my server and crucifer and now seminary student Mr. Lou Townsend on this issue. We were sipping over a cup of hot tea at my kitchen table not long ago. In the liturgical traditions such as the Roman, Anglican, Orthodox and Lutheran denominations, the members enter the church seeking reconciliation with God and forgiveness of sins that typically culminate with participation in the Holy Eucharist. Far too many Protestant services enter worship services to learn about the lessons of Scripture and how they are to live and to find ways to feel good about themselves from the sermon and music. The difference between liturgical services and non-liturgical services is centered-on which party is the giver and which party is the receiver. The non-liturgical groups give offerings

---

[241] Disciple's Study Bible, The. (1988) The Disciple's Study Bible. *The Disciple's Study Bible New International Version.* Holman Bible Publishers. A Cornerstone Bible. Nashville, Tennessee. The Old Testament. King Solomon. The Book of Ecclesiastes 3:1-8. Pages 791-792. Matthew. The Gospel of Matthew 22:14. Pages 433.

but expect automatic knowledge or grace in return. The liturgical groups bring alms and oblations but do not expect a return of knowledge or grace or even blessings until they first reconcile with God. So it seems one group believes they are justified to receive grace, absolution and blessings and consequently take them for granted; while the other group enters the worship service with a repentant heart while seeking reconciliation, forgiveness and redemption and thus receiving grace, absolution and blessings that is not automatic. The one group expects the grace while the other group expects the grace but recognizes that it is conditional on repentance. One group believes they automatically have a chair at the table while the other group believes they do not deserve the crumbs under the table so to speak.

This is a theological understanding that is not easy to explain. I find that it is as difficult as trying to explain why St. John calls Jesus the 'Word'.[242] I am not the only one who has had difficulty trying to explain a difficult theological issue nor will I be the last. Indeed, my lawyer friend and Anglican Deacon Mac Tyson once said in a Sunday school lesson, 'sometimes it is easier to explain why something is not, rather than to explain why something is.' So, please indulge me as I will try to explain this again and this time I will explain in the form of a parable as Christ often did. The saying, 'once saved, always saved' is only half the lesson. Many so-called Christians take this statement to heart and then live a very sinful life thinking they are exempt from judgment. 'Once saved, always saved' is true but it is only half-true. For this to work, you must amend your behavior and strive to cease your sinful practices and behavior as you once lived, and then lead a new life. If you continue to live as you did before, or you do not turn your life around, then as a priest I hope you see the light before it is too late. I invite the reader to read the *Parable of the Sower* to clarify this lesson. Another good parable which shows us the truth is the *Parable of the Ten Virgins*. You can lose your 'religion' and many do as some

---

[242] Holy Bible, The. (2004). The Holy Bible. *The Holy Bible Authorized King James Version*. World Publishing. Nashville, Tennessee. www.worldpublishing.com. St. John. The Gospel of John 1:1. Page 467.

see it. More than likely you never had 'religion' to start with. Jesus Christ tells us in the gospel of St.

Matthew that we should *'enter by the narrow gate; for wide is the gate and broad is the way that leads to destruction, and there are many who go in by it. Because narrow is the gate and difficult is the way which leads to life, and there are few who find it.'*[243] Few who find it should be our wakeup call. We can either choose to live for God in sacred theism or live for Satan in secular humanism. There is no other way. Those who try to straddle the two ways end up losing both ways.

Again, this is why the *Articles of Religion* are so important and a key staple in the *Pentagon of Faith*. If you worship in a non-liturgical denomination, you have largely lost a tradition that encompasses the worship service in the form of vestments, the omission of the processional and the recessional, the use of candles, the censing of the altar, and most importantly, the regular participation in the Holy Eucharist. In the Gospel of Luke we read, *'This is my body which is given for you: do this in remembrance of Me.'*[244] If we all return to the traditional faith and practices of our fathers, we will see a dramatic change in the way we worship and the results will be evident in our society and the civilized world. Regular participation in the sacrament of Holy Communion will go a long way to restoring our relationship with God, our Creator and Redeemer. This would be a small step and large leap for the believer either to turn or return to a life and practice of sacred theism and depart from a life and practice of secular humanism. The *Articles of Religion* can and will help the believer understand the fundamentals of the Christian faith along their spiritual journey for we are spirits created for eternity and are only flesh and bones for a few short years.

---

[243] Believer's Study Bible, The. (1991). The Believer's Study Bible. *The Believer's Study Bible New King James Version.* Thomas Nelson Publishers. Nashville, Tennessee. The New Testament. St. Matthew. The Gospel of Matthew 7:13-14. Page 1347.

[244] Believer's Study Bible, The. (1991). The Believer's Study Bible. *The Believer's Study Bible New King James Version.* Thomas Nelson Publishers. Nashville, Tennessee. The New Testament. St. Luke. The Gospel of Luke 22:19. Page 1481.

The American version of the *Articles of Religion* is found in the Anglican Book of Common Prayer. As a point of reference to all Christians, since I am an Anglican priest, I remind the reader that I use these articles as a starting point. If and when there is need to discuss other denominational views, when they vary, then I will make notation of that difference. And although there are areas of differences, we must always keep mindful that there is more that binds us as Christians than separates us. In Ephesians 4:5, we learn we have one Father of us all and we still have 'one Lord, one faith, one baptism'. We also have our Lord and Savior Jesus Christ, and His Father our Heavenly Father as well as the Holy Spirit who dwells within us.

The Thirty-Nine Articles of Religion:

I. *Of Faith in the Holy Trinity.*

Therefore is but one living and true God, everlasting, without body, parts, or passions; of infinite power, wisdom, and goodness; the Maker, and Preserver of all things both visible and invisible. And in unity of this Godhead there be three Persons, of one substance, power, and eternity; the Father, the Son, and the Holy Ghost.

<u>Authors Note:</u> *This is the most fundamental doctrine of the Christian faith and what separates us from the other religions of the world. The three persons in one is a paradox which cannot be explained; that is why it is called a paradox. Here we have God the Father, God the Son and God the Holy Spirit. We believe this because of our faith, as stated in Hebrews 11:1. "Now faith is the substance of things hoped for, the evidence of things not seen."*

II. *Of the Word or Son of God, which was made very Man*

The Son, which is the Word of the Father, begotten from everlasting of the Father, the very and eternal God, and of one substance with the Father, took Man's nature in the womb of the blessed Virgin, of her substance; so that two whole and perfect Natures, that is to say, the Godhead and the Manhood, were joined together in one Person, never to be divided, whereof is one Christ, very God, and very Man; who truly suffered, was crucified, dead, and buried, to reconcile his Father to us, and to be a sacrifice, not only for original guilt, but also for actual sins of men.

<u>Author's note:</u> Christ's virgin birth is often challenged by unbelievers and naysayers. This is at the core of our Christian doctrine and beliefs. It confirms the omnipotence, omniscience, and omnipresence of God our Creator and redeemer, and Heavenly Father who made Christ incarnate. Jesus Christ is the propitiation or perfect sacrifice for the sins of the whole world. By His death, He enables the atonement of our sins.

III. *Of the Going down of Christ into Hell.*

As Christ died for us, and was buried; so also is it to believed, that he went down into Hell.

<u>Author's note:</u> Some Christians omit Christ descending into hell and defeating death and Satan as in the reciting of the Apostle's Creed. However, it is very much a part of our Christian belief and should be taught because it reveals that there is a real devil and there is a

real hell and we have a choice where we spend our eternity in one place or the other. Hell is described as a place of departed spirits, or a place of eternal damnation or punishment, or a place that is absent of God. Whichever view of hell you choose will not change the fact that it is not a place you wish to spend eternity. It is a place of sadness, pain, suffering, and sorrows.

IV. *Of the Resurrection of Christ.*

Christ did truly rise again from death, and took again his body, with flesh, bones, and all things appertaining to the perfection of Man's nature; wherewith he ascended into Heaven, and there sittith, until he return to judge all man at the last day.

<u>Author's note</u>: There are those who say that no one can return from the dead. These naysayers have said this from the beginning of time. By His death on the cross, Jesus Christ descended into hell where He defeated sin and overcame death and rose again on the third day. Christ paid for our sins and one day we will live with Christ for eternity in heaven. As we read in I Corinthians 15:42-49, "So also is the resurrection of the dead. The body is sown in corruption, it is raised in incorruption. It is sown in dishonor, it is raised in glory. It is sown in weakness, it is raised in power. It is sown a natural body, it is raised a spiritual body. There is a natural body and there is a spiritual body. And so it is written, 'the first man Adam became a living being', the last Adam became a life giving spirit. However, the spiritual is not first, but the natural, and afterward the spiritual. The first man was of

the earth, made of dust; the second Man is the Lord from heaven. As was the man of dust, so also are those who are made of dust; and as is the heavenly Man, so also are those who are heavenly. And as we have borne the image of the man of dust, we shall also bear the image of the heavenly Man".

V. *Of the Holy Ghost.*

The Holy Ghost, proceeding from the Father and the Son, is of one substance, majesty, and glory, with the Father and the Son, very and eternal God.

<u>Author's note</u>: The Holy Ghost is a part of the Holy Trinity consisting of God the Father, God the Son, and God the Holy Spirit. He is the comforter whom Christ sent to dwell among us in our bodies which are the temple of God. As we read in John 14: 15-18, "If you love Me, keep my commandments. And I will pray the Father, and He will give you another Helper, that He may abide with you forever—the Spirit of truth whom the world cannot receive, because it neither sees Him nor knows Him; but you know Him, for He dwells with you and will be in you. I will not leave you orphans; I will come to you".

VI. *Of the Sufficiency of the Holy Scriptures for Salvation.*

Holy Scripture containeth all things necessary for salvation: so that whatsoever is not read therein, nor may be proved thereby, is not to be required of any man, that it should be believed as an article of Faith, or be thought requisite or necessary to salvation. In the name of the Holy Scripture we do understand those canonical Books of the Old and New Testament, of whose authority was never any doubt in the Church. Of the Names and Number of Canonical Books, Genesis, Exodus, Leviticus, Numbers, Deuteronomy, Joshua, Judges, Ruth, I Samuel, II Samuel, I Kings, II Kings, I Chronicles, II Chronicles, I Esdras, II Esdras, Esther, Job, Psalms, Proverbs, Ecclesiastes or Preacher, Cantica of Song of Solomon, Four Prophets the Greater, Twelve Prophets the less. And the other Books (as Hierome saith) the Church doth read for example of life and instruction of manners; but yet doth it not apply them to establish any doctrine; such are these following: III Esdras, IV Esdras, Tobias, Judith, the rest of the Book of Esther, Wisdom, Jesus the Son of Sirach, Baruch the Prophet, Song of the Three Children, Story of Susanna, Of Bel and the Dragon, Prayer of Manasses, I Maccabees, II Maccabees. All the Books of the New Testament, as they are commonly received, we do receive, and account them Canonical.

Author's note: The Holy Scriptures are the inspired Word of God and all things necessary for salvation are included in them. As they are written, no one should attempt to rewrite the Scriptures or they may face severe consequences. These other books mentioned in this article are known as the Apocrypha. Some churches accept them as canonical while others do not.

VII. Of the Old Testament.

The Old Testament is not contrary to the New: for both in the Old and New Testament everlasting Life is offered to Mankind by Christ, who is the only Mediator between God and Man, being both God and Man. Wherefore they are not to be heard, which feign that the old Fathers did look only for transitory promises. Although the Law given from God by Moses, as touching Ceremonies and Rites, do not bind Christian men, nor the Civil precepts thereof ought of necessity to be received in any commonwealth; yet notwithstanding, no Christian man whatsoever is free from the obedience of the Commandments which are called Moral.

Author's note: The Holy Bible is about God's relationship with His greatest creation, Man. The Old Testament sets the stage for the New Testament. Some scholars have described the Old Testament as the youthful man while the New Testament is described as the mature man. All the books in the Holy Scriptures from Genesis to Revelation tell the greatest love story ever told.

VIII. Of the Creeds.

The Nicene Creed and that which is commonly called the Apostle's Creed ought thoroughly to be received and believed: for they may be proved by most certain warrants of Holy Scripture.

Author's note: The Athanasian Creed is omitted here in this article because all the necessary points in Christianity are already made in the Apostles and Nicene Creeds. The Athanasian Creed is used most notably by the Orthodox Church. It is recognized as one of the three primary Christian Creeds and is included in the second segment of Part Two.

IX. *Of Original or Birth-Sin.*

Original sin standeth not in the following of Adam, (as the Pelagians do vainly talk;) but it is the fault and corruption of the Nature of every man, that naturally is engendered of the offspring of Adam; whereby man is very far gone from original righteousness, and of his own nature inclined to evil, so that the flesh lusteth always contrary to the Spirit; and therefore in every person born into this world it deserveth God's wrath and damnation. And this infection of nature doth remain, yea in them that are regenerated; whereby the lust of the flesh, called in Greek frovnhma sarkovß, (which some do expound the wisdom, some sensuality, some the affection, some the desire, of the flesh,) is not subject to the Law of God. And although there is no condemnation for them that believe and are baptized; yet the Apostle doth confess that concupiscence and lust hath of itself the nature of sin.

<u>Author note</u>: We are all born of original sin or birthsin and are unable of <u>ourselves</u> to save ourselves from God's judgment.

X. *Of Free-Will.*

The condition of Man after the fall of Adam is such that he cannot turn and prepare himself, by his own natural strength and good works, to faith, and calling upon God. Wherefore we have no power to do good works pleasant and acceptable to God, without the grace of God by Christ preventing us, that we have a good will and working with us, when we have that good will.

Author's note: God gave us our free will. It is our free will to accept or reject His Son as our Savior. If we did not have free will, and God decided on our behalf to believe in Him, then what purpose would there be for Him to create a hell for the unbelievers? The grace of God goes before our good works. In the 16th century, the word *prevent* meant to go before as it is translated from Latin into English.

XI. Of the Justification of Man.

We are accounted righteous before God, only for the merit of our Lord and Savior Jesus Christ by Faith, and not for our own works or deserving's. Wherefore that we are justified by Faith only, is a most wholesome Doctrine, and very full of comfort, as more largely is expressed in the Homily of Justification.

Author's note: Some Christian communions have considered for centuries that works and faith were a means of grace. However, all Catholic and Protestant communions now consider justification to be by faith only. Indeed, we bear witness to our justification from the evidence of our work by Christ in thought, word, and deed.

XII. Of Good Works.

Albeit that Good Works, which are the fruits of Faith, and follow after Justification, cannot put away our sins, and endure the severity of God's judgment; yet are they pleasing and acceptable to God in Christ, and do spring out necessarily of a true and lively Faith; insomuch that by them a lively Faith may be as evidently known as a tree discerned by the fruit.

<u>Author's note</u>: Again, we are justified only by faith. Good works alone will not get us into heaven. However, our works and good deeds represent the level of our faith. They are the fruits of our spirit. God sees all that we do both the good and the bad. In James 2:14, 17-18 we read, "What does it profit, my brethren, if someone says he has faith but does not have works? Can faith save him?…Thus also faith by itself, if it does not have works, is dead. But someone will say, 'you have faith, and I have works'. Show me your faith without your works and I will show you my faith by my works."

XIII. Of Works before Justification.

Works done before the grace of Christ, and the Inspiration of his Spirit, are not pleasant to God, forasmuch as they spring not of faith in Jesus Christ; neither do they make men meet to receive grace, or (as the School-authors say) deserve grace of congruity: yea rather for that they are not done as God hath willed and commanded them to be done, we doubt not but they have the nature of sin.

<u>Author's note</u>: Good deeds or works are not pleasant to God if they do not spring from the love of Christ in our lives. As a footnote, the School-authors were also known as the Scholastics.

XIV. Of Works of Supererogation[245].

Voluntary Works besides, over and above, God's Commandments, which they call Works of Supererogation, cannot be taught without arrogance and impiety: for by them men do declare, that they do not only render unto God as much as they are bound to do, but that they do more for his sake, than of bounden duty is required whereas Christ saith plainly, When ye have done all that are commanded to you, say, We are unprofitable servants.

<u>Author's note</u>: The Apostle Paul tells us that we believe because of our faith. However, our faith is dead unless we support it with good works. Works alone will not grant us entrance into heaven. We must first repent of our sins and accept Christ as our Lord and Savior. Our bounden duty to God requires total commitment of all that we are and all that we have. Anything less is unacceptable.

XV. Of Christ alone without Sin.

Christ in the truth of our nature was made like unto us in all things, sin only except, from which he was clearly void, both in his flesh and in his spirit. He came to be the Lamb without spot who, by sacrifice of himself once made, should take away the sins of the world; and sin (as Saint John saith) was not in him. But all we the rest, although baptized, and born again in Christ, yet offend in

---

[245] Supererogation. (2001) Random House College Dictionary. *Random House Webster's College Dictionary 2nd Revised and Updated.* Random House, Inc. New York, New York. www.randomhouse.com. Page 1314.

many things; and if we say we have no sin, we deceive ourselves, and the truth is not in us.

<u>Author's note</u>: The only perfect man without sin was Jesus Christ. Anyone who claims they are without sin deceives himself.

XV. *Of Sin after Baptism.*

Not every deadly sin willingly committed after Baptism is sin against the Holy Ghost, and unpardonable. Wherefore the grant of repentance is not to be denied to such as fall into sin after Baptism. After we have received the Holy Ghost, we may depart from grace given and fall into sin, and by the grace of God we may arise again, and amend our lives. And therefore they are to be condemned, which say, they can no more sin as long, as they live here, or deny the place of forgiveness to such as truly repent.

<u>Author's note</u>: The spirit is willing but the flesh is weak. All the more reason we should attend regular worship service; and truly and earnestly repent and find reconciliation in Christ Jesus. For all have sinned and fallen short of the glory of God. The unpardonable sin is the unbelief in Jesus Christ.

XVI. *Of Predestination and Election.*

Predestination to Life is the everlasting purpose of God, whereby (before the foundations of the world were laid) he hath constantly decreed by his counsel secret to us, to deliver from curse and damnation those whom he hath chosen in Christ out of mankind, and to bring them by

Christ to everlasting salvation, as vessels made to honor. Wherefore they which be endued with so excellent a benefit of God, be called according to God's purpose by his Spirit working in due season: they through Grace obey the calling: they be justified freely: they be made sons of God by adoption: they be made like the image of his only begotten Son Jesus Christ; they walk religiously in good works, and at length, by God's mercy, they attain to everlasting felicity.

As the godly consideration of Predestination, and our Election in Christ, is full of sweet, pleasant, and unspeakable comfort to godly persons, and such as feel in themselves the working of the Spirit of Christ, mortifying the works of the flesh, and their earthly members, and drawing up their mind to high and heavenly things, as well because it doth greatly establish and confirm their faith of eternal Salvation to be enjoyed through Christ, as because it doth fervently kindle their love towards God; So, for curious and carnal persons, lacking the Spirit of Christ, to have continually before their eyes the sentence of God's Predestination, is a most dangerous downfall, whereby the Devil doth thrust them either into desperation, or into wretchlessness of most unclean living, no less perilous than desperation.

Furthermore, we must receive God's promises in such wise, as thy be generally set forth to us in Holy Scripture; and, in our doing, that Will of God is to be followed, which we have expressly declared unto us in the Word of God.

<u>Author's note</u>: God our Creator knew us before we were born. He is also the Alpha and the

Omega.[246] No doubt He knows who will spend eternity with Him or who will not. If we live by the teachings and commandments of God and Jesus Christ which we learn in the Holy Scriptures, then we will fulfill God's purpose for us and we will live for eternity in heaven with Him.

XVIII. Of obtaining eternal Salvation only by the Name of Christ.

They also are to be had accursed that presume to say that every man shall be saved by the Law or Sect which he professeth, so that he be diligent to frame his life according to that Law and the light of Nature. For Holy Scripture doth set out unto us only the Name of Jesus Christ, whereby men must be saved.

<u>Author's note</u>: There is only one way for salvation, and that is through the belief in Jesus Christ as Lord and Savior. We are able to reach the Father only through His Son. In St. Luke 10:22 we read, "All things have been delivered to Me by My Father, and no one knows who the Son is except the Father, and who the Father is except the Son, and the one to whom the Son wills to reveal Him".

XIX. Of the Church.

The visible Church is a congregation of faithful men, in the which the pure Word of God is

---

[246] Holy Bible, The. (2004). The Holy Bible. *The Holy Bible Authorized King James Version.* World Publishing. Nashville, Tennessee. www.worldpublishing.com. St. John. The Book of Revelation 1:8. Page 544.

preached, and the Sacraments be duly ministered according to Christ's ordinance, in all those things that of necessity are requisite to the same. As the Church of Jerusalem, Alexandria, and Antioch, have erred; so also the Church of Rome hath erred, not only in their living and manner of Ceremonies, but also in matters of Faith.

Author's note: This was written during the heat of the Protestant Reformation and certainly there was an abundance of misdeeds on the side of the Roman Catholic Church. In the subsequent centuries, cooperation and reconciliation has been the order of the day and realizing the Summary of the Law, fellow Christians have found a way to relate to each other, thanks be to God.

XX. Of Authority of the Church.

The Church hath power to decree Rites or Ceremonies, and authority in Controversies of Faith: and yet it is not lawful for the Church to ordain anything that is contrary to God's Word written neither may it so expound one place of Scripture, that it be repugnant to another. Wherefore, although the Church be a witness and a keeper of Holy Writ, yet, as it ought not to decree any thing against the same, so besides the same ought it not to enforce any thing to be believed for necessity of salvation.

Author's note: The Holy Scriptures are the final authority in all matters that concern the Church including rites and ceremonies as well as the administration of the church. The Church is the defender of the faith. It is not proper for any outside educational or governmental body to interfere.

XXI. *Of the Authority of General Councils.*

(The Twenty-first of the former Articles is omitted; because it is partly of a local and civil nature, and is provided for, as to the remaining parts of it, in other Articles.)

XXII. *Of Purgatory.*

The Romish Doctrine concerning Purgatory, Pardon, and Worshipping and Adoration, as well of Images as of Relics, and also Invocation of Saints, is a fond thing, vainly invented, and grounded upon no warranty of Scripture, but rather repugnant to the Word of God.

<u>Author's note</u>: These Protestant views were at odds with the Roman Catholic Church during the Protestant Reformation concerning clerical abuses. Obviously, Christians do not or should not worship the relic, the statue, the icon, the saint, or the cross but we should honor or venerate who that image represents in the Name of Our Lord Jesus Christ and our Heavenly Father. We do honor those Christians and Apostles whose lives are exemplary for having successfully 'fought the good fight.'[247] Acknowledging their contributions to Christianity is no different than recognizing

---

[247] Holy Bible, The. (2004). The Holy Bible. *The Holy Bible Authorized King James Version.* World Publishing. Nashville, Tennessee. www.worldpublishing.com. St. Paul. The Second Epistle of Paul to Timothy 4:7. Page 529.

the signers of the United States Constitution or our U. S. Presidents for their service to this country. Regarding purgatory, there is no basis in Scripture to support this doctrine.

XXIII. Of Ministering in the Congregation.

It is not lawful for any man to take upon him the office of public preaching, or ministering the Sacrament in the Congregation, before he is lawfully called, and sent to execute the same. And those we ought to judge lawfully called and sent, which be chosen and called to this work by men who have public authority given unto them in the Congregation, to call and send Ministers into the Lord's vineyard.

Author's note: Preaching or administering the sacraments as vocations that should not be taken by one who is not validly ordained. In most communions, one is required to have a valid license to officiate just as in any other vocation that requires advanced training such as law or medicine to hold a license.

XXIV. Of Speaking in the Congregation in such a Tongue as the people understandeth.

It is a thing plainly repugnant to the Word of God, and the custom of the Primitive Church, to have public Prayer in the Church, or to minister the Sacrament, in a tongue not understood of the people.

Author's note: This article is written to address the Roman Catholic Latin Mass which would not be understood by anyone who did not speak the language. It is completely appropriate and necessary that everyone understand the words used in the entire service.

XXV. *Of the Sacraments.*

Sacraments ordained of Christ be not only badges or tokens of Christian men's profession, but rather they be certain sure witnesses, and effectual signs of grace, and God's good will towards us, by the which he doth work invisibly in us, and doth not only quicken, but also strengthen and confirm our Faith in Him. There are two Sacraments ordained of Christ our Lord in the Gospel, that is to say, Baptism, and the Supper of the Lord. Those five commonly called Sacraments, that is to say, Confirmation, Penance, Orders, Matrimony, and Extreme Unction, are not to be counted for Sacraments of the Gospel being such as have grown partly of the corrupt following of the Apostles, partly are states of life allowed in the Scriptures; but yet have not like nature of Sacraments with Baptism and the Lord's Supper, for that they have not any visible sign of ceremony ordained of God. The Sacraments were not ordained of Christ to be gazed upon, or to be carried about, but that we should duly use them. And in such only as worthily receive the same, they have a wholesome effect of operation: but they that receive them unworthily, purchase to themselves damnation, as Saith Paul saith.

<u>Author's note</u>: The seven Sacraments, two major and five minor, are addressed in the fourth segment of Part Two. However, I might draw your attention to the end of the third sentence

which says 'ordained of God'. No doubt Holy Baptism and Holy Communion are specifically mentioned in the Scriptures as ordained of God. The lesser five sacraments are referred to in the Scripture but are not ordained of God. This article seems to discourage observance of the five lesser sacraments stating they have grown partly of the corrupt following of the Apostles. They are no less important to our traditional Christian worship. I also describe the outward and visible sign and inward and spiritual grace as I understand and view it in the fourth segment.

XXVI. Of the Unworthiness of the Ministers, which hinders not the effect of the Sacraments.

Although in the visible Church the evil be ever mingled with the good, and sometime the evil have chief authority in the Ministration of the Word and Sacraments, yet forasmuch as they do not the same in their own name, but in Christ's, and do minister by his commission and authority, we may use their Ministry, both in hearing the Word of God, and in receiving the Sacraments. Neither is the effect of Christ's ordinance taken away by their wickedness, nor the grace of God's gifts diminished from such as by Faith and rightly, do receive the Sacraments ministered unto them; which be effectual, because of Christ's institution and promise, although they be ministered by evil men. Nevertheless, it appertaineth to the discipline of the Church, that inquiry be made of evil Ministers, and that they be accused by those that have knowledge of their offenses; and finally, being found guilty, by just judgment be deposed.

Author's note: All sacraments are administered in Christ's name, not in the name of the celebrant. If an unworthy minister celebrates a sacrament, it is still valid for it is administered in Christ's name and Jesus Christ is the celebrant.

XXVII. Of Baptism.

Baptism is not only a sign of profession, and mark of difference, whereby Christian men are discerned from others that be not christened, but it is also a sign of Regeneration or New-Birth, whereby as by an instrument, they that receive Baptism rightly are grafted into the Church; the promises of the forgiveness of sin, and of our adoption to be the sons of God by the Holy Ghost, are visibly signed and sealed; Faith is confirmed, and Grace increased by virtue of prayer unto God.

The Baptism of young Children is in any wise to be retained in the Church, as most agreeable with the institution of Christ.

Author's note: Again, Holy Baptism is addressed in the fourth segment of Part Two.

XXVIII. Of the Lord's Supper.

The Supper of the Lord is not only a sign of the love that Christians ought to have among themselves one to another; but rather it is a Sacrament of our Redemption by Christ's death: insomuch that to such as rightly, worthily, and with faith, receive the same, the Bread which we break is a partaking of the Body of Christ; and likewise the Cup of Blessing is a partaking of the Blood of Christ.

Transubstantiation (or the change of the substance of Bread and Wine) in the Supper of the Lord cannot be proved by Holy Writ; but is repugnant to the plain words of Scripture, overthroweth the nature of a Sacrament, and hath given occasion to many superstitions.

The Body of Christ is given, taken, and eaten, in the Supper, only after an heavenly and spiritual manner. And the mean whereby the Body of Christ is received and eaten in the Supper, is Faith.

The sacrament of the Lord's Supper was not by Christ's ordinance reserved, carried about, lifted up, or worshipped.

Author's note: The Holy Communion, the Lord's Supper, and the Holy Eucharist all being the same, are discussed in detail in the fourth segment of Part Two.

XXIX. *Of the Wicked, which eat not the Body of Christ in the use of the Lord's Supper.*

The Wicked, and such as be void of a lively faith, although they do carnally and visibly press with their teeth (as Saint Augustine saith) the Sacrament of the Body and Blood of Christ; yet in no wise are they partakers of Christ: but rather, to their condemnation, do eat and drink the sign or Sacrament of so great a thing.

Author's note: The Lord's Supper is only for those baptized Christians who have repented and sought reconciliation with God. Anyone who is not a baptized Christian, and chooses to receive the consecrated elements according to the Scriptures risks damnation in hell. The practice of some communions to limit their membership the full participation in communion would seem to run counter to the proclamation of God's love as expressed in the Holy Scriptures.

XXX. *Of both Kinds.*

The Cup of the Lord is not to be denied to the Laypeople; for both the parts of the Lord's Sacrament, by Christ's ordinance and commandment, ought to be ministered to all Christian men alike.

Author's note: The bread and the wine are to be offered to the communicant at the altar. However, the consuming of either or the other is sufficient to constitute a valid communion. The avoidance of one element does not invalidate a reception of communion.

XXXI. *Of the one Oblation of Christ finished upon the Cross.*

The offering of Christ once made is that perfect redemption, propitiation, and satisfaction, for all sins of the whole world, both original and actual; and there is none other satisfaction for sin, but that alone. Wherefore the sacrifices of Masses, in the which it was commonly said, that the Priest did offer Christ for the quick and the dead, to have remission of pain or guilt, were blasphemous fables, and dangerous deceits.

Author's note: Jesus Christ's blood is the only price God will accept for the remission of the sins of the whole world. Those who reject

Jesus Christ as Savior simultaneously reject the atonement for their sins and will suffer the divine judgment.

XXXII. Of the Marriage of Priests.[248]

Bishops, Priests, and Deacons, are not commanded by God's law, either to vow the estate of single life, or to abstain from marriage: therefore it is lawful for them, as for all other Christian men, to marry at their own discretion, as they shall judge the same to serve better to godliness.

<u>Author's note</u>: The Roman Catholic Church does not allow priests to marry although ironically in the early centuries of the church, it was permitted. The Anglican Church does allow the marriage of priests as does the Orthodox Church if the priest was married before entering the priesthood.

XXXIII. Of excommunicate Persons, how they are to be avoided.

That person which by open denunciation of the Church is rightly cut off from the unity of the Church, and excommunicated, ought to be taken of the whole multitude of the faithful, as an Heathen and Publican, until he be openly reconciled by penance, and received into the Church by a Judge that hath authority thereunto.

<u>Author's note</u>: Only bishops have the authority to excommunicate. Christians should be

---

[248] Holy Bible, The. (2004). The Holy Bible. *The Holy Bible Authorized King James Version.* World Publishing. Nashville, Tennessee. www.worldpublishing.com. The Old Testament. Moses. The Book of Leviticus 21:1-24. Page 60.

careful with whom we associate lest we become like them and fall away from our sacred theistic lives and delve into a life of secular humanism. Christians should also continue to pray for our fallen brothers and sisters in hope that they may depart from their wayward ways and return to the fold.

XXXIV. Of the Traditions of the Church.

It is not necessary that Traditions and Ceremonies be in all places one, or utterly like; for at all times they have been divers, and may be changed according to the diversity of countries, times, and men's manners, so that nothing be ordained against God's Word. Whosoever, through his private judgment, willingly and purposely, doth openly break the Traditions and Ceremonies of the Church, which be not repugnant to the Word of God, and be ordained and approved by common authority, ought to be rebuked openly, (that others may fear to do the like,) as he that offendeth against the common order of the Church, and hurteth the authority of the Magistrate, and woundeth the consciences of the weak brethren. Every particular or national Church hath authority to ordain, change and abolish, Ceremonies or Rites of the Church ordained only by man's authority, so that all things be done to edifying.

<u>Author's note</u>: As I have pointed out in this book, the pendulum has swung too far to the secular humanist position and a balance needs to be struck by returning to the traditional faith of our fathers as they practiced and worshipped in a sacred theistic way.

XXXV. Of the Homilies.

The Second Book of Homilies, the several titles whereof we have joined under this Article, doth contain a godly and wholesome Doctrine, and necessary for these times, as doth the former Book of Homilies, which were set forth in the time of Edward the Sixth; and therefore we judge them to be read in Churches by the Ministers, diligently and distinctly, that they may be understood of the people. Of the Names of the homilies: 1. Of the right Use of the Church. 2. Against Peril of Idolatry. 3. Of repairing and keeping clean of Churches. 4. Of good Works: first of Fasting. 5. Against Gluttony and Drunkenness. 6. Against Excess of Apparel. 7. Of Prayer. 8. Of the Place and Time of Prayer. 9. That Common Prayers and Sacraments ought to be ministered in a known tongue. 10. Of the reverend Estimation of God's Word. 11. Of Almsdoing. 12. Of the Nativity of Christ. 13. Of the Passion of Christ. 14. Of the Resurrection of Christ. 15. Of the worthy receiving of the Sacrament of the Body and Blood of Christ. 16. Of the Gifts of the Holy Ghost. 17. For the Rogation-days. 18. Of the State of Matrimony. 19. Of Repentance. 20. Against Idleness. 21. Against Rebellion. (This Article is received in this Church, so far as it declares the Book of Homilies to be an explication of Christian doctrine, and instructive in piety and morals. But all references to the constitution and laws of England are considered as inapplicable to the circumstances of this Church; which also suspends the order for the reading of said Homilies in churches, until a revision of them may be conveniently made, for the clearing of them, as well from obsolete words and phrases, as from the local references.)

Author's note: Homilies and sermons are vitally important to the spiritual welfare of the Church. In our liturgical tradition we administer and celebrate both the Word and the Sacrament. A member of the clergy should be well versed in the Holy Scriptures so as not to border on any false doctrine or apostasy at all times when ministering to God's people. The *Book of Homilies* is a collection of sermons useful for the guidance of both the clergy and laity on the subject listed. The first *Book of Homily* was published in 1547 while the second *Book of Homily* was published in 1562.

XXXVI. Of Consecration of Bishops and Ministers.

The Book of Consecration of Bishops, and Ordering of Priests and Deacons, as set forth by the General Convention of this Church in 1792, doth contain all things necessary to such Consecration and Ordering; neither hath it anything that of itself is superstitious and ungodly. And, therefore, whosoever are consecrated or ordered according to said Form, we decree all such to be rightly, orderly, and lawfully consecrated and ordered.

Author's note: The Book of Common Prayer includes a section called the Ordinal which describes the service of consecrating and ordaining bishops, priests, and deacons. The Apostolic Succession which was ordained and instituted by Jesus Christ was established with His Twelve Apostles before His Ascension. The succession represents an unbroken chain of laying on of hands in the sacrament of Holy Orders for all clergy who are called to the order.

XXXVII. Of the Power of the Civil Magistrates.

The Power of the Civil Magistrate extendeth to all men, as well Clergy as Laity, in all things temporal; but hath no authority in things purely spiritual. And we hold it to be the duty of all men who are professors of the Gospel, to pay respectful obedience to the Civil Authority, regularly and legitimately constituted.

<u>Author's note</u>: This article denies the validity of separate judicial systems for clergy and laity but affirms the right of the church to try purely spiritual matters. In other words, clergy are subject to civil laws.

XXXVIII. Of Christian Men's Goods, which are not common.

The Riches and Goods of Christians are not common, as touching the right, title, and possession of the same; as certain Anabaptists do falsely boast. Notwithstanding, every man ought, of such things as he possesseth, liberally to give alms to the poor, according to his ability.

<u>Authors' note</u>: Christ said it is better to give than receive. Anabaptists, as well as other sects, who grew out of the Protestant Reformation believed in the common holding of all material goods and the equal distribution of the same.

XXXIX. Of a Christian Man's Oath.

As we confess that vain and rash Swearing is forbidden Christian men by our Lord Jesus Christ, and James his Apostle, so we judge that Christian Religion doth not prohibit, but that a man may swear when the Magistrate requireth, in a cause of faith and charity, so it be done according to the Prophet's teaching, in justice, judgment, and truth.

<u>Author's note</u>: This last article speaks to the commandment that we do not bear false witness concerning our fellow man. Our oath is our bond. Every utterance from our mouths is recorded in the book of life. Swearing is prohibited of a Christian man except in cases of justice, judgment and truth.

In Conclusion

It is fairly clear that our nation and world is headed in the wrong direction when it comes to our Christian faith, biblical morality, and traditional forms of worship. Some people believe we need a revival of our spirit. We seem to have lost our way and we are sailing without a rudder or compass. I believe we need a revival that is sustainable. Unfortunately, far more than less Christians get caught up in the heat of the moment and soon cool off and fade away. We identified the world of secular humanism in this book and established that there is a critical need to return to practicing the tenets and virtues of a life of sacred theism.

In St. Luke's Gospel[249], Christ gave us the *Parable of the Sower*, as well as in St. Matthew chapter 13 and St. Mark chapter 4. The fact that all three synoptic Gospels include this parable indicates that it is of the highest level of importance to Christians. In this parable Christ describes four types of soils and we can correlate this to mean four types of Christians. The first soil is wayward and it is easily trampled underfoot and eaten by birds for the Word of God soon falls on deaf ears. This is the so-called Christian who hears the salvation story but fails to act on it. The second soil is rock and the seeds that are broadcast begin to grow but because they are undernourished, they sprout up but in the heat of the day causes them to wither away. This is the so-called Christian who is looking for the warm and fuzzy feeling that when it fades, he begins to fade away in his daily devotion and attendance to church

---

[249] Holy Bible, The. (2004). The Holy Bible. *The Holy Bible Authorized King James Version.* World Publishing. Nashville, Tennessee. www.world.publishing.com. The New Testament. St. Luke. The Gospel of Luke 8:4-15. Pages 1451-1452.

services and eventually stops worshipping and attending church services altogether. The third soil is thorny and when the seeds mature, so do the thorns of the vines and they wrap around the tender plant and eventually choke it to death.

This so-called Christian is the one who makes a valiant effort to live the Christian life of praise and worship for a while but eventually gets wrapped up in the cares of this world and soon finds no more time to attend church services. Thereafter he becomes a victim to his or her worldly desires. The fourth is the good soil which was properly nourished. The plant grew up strong and produced fruit many times its weight. This is symbolic of the one true Christian who continues to persevere against the vices and temptations of this world. This is the Christian who follows God's commandments and regularly finds time to worship and serve God every way he or she can on a daily basis. The other three so-called Christians had a desire to be a Christian but were unwilling or unable to follow God's commandments. They ultimately chose to live for themselves instead of living for God.

In an earlier short story I wrote about an urban legend that claimed Dr. Billy Graham may have said that there are two out of ten Christians who are true Christians which accounts to one in five. Dr. D. James Kennedy is reported to have claimed that there are millions who claim to be Christian but their lives reflect the opposite. In the *Parable of the Sower*, we realize that this story represents one in four. If we look at the *Parable of the Ten Virgins*,[250] we see that the ratio is one out of every two. Christ tells us that the gate to enter heaven is a narrow gate that few will find. These numbers should be sobering statistics and I would hope a wakeup call for those Christians who take their relationship with God so casually. We should examine ourselves to determine in which category of soil we find ourselves living.

Like the Brotherhood of St. Andrew, whose motto is Prayer, Study, and Service, we must make these tenets our guiding

---

[250] Holy Bible, The. (2004). The Holy Bible. *The Holy Bible Authorized King James Version*. World Publishing. Nashville, Tennessee. www.worldpublishing.com. The New Testament. St. Matthew. The Gospel of Matthew 25:1-13. Page 434.

principle in our lives. We must be disciplined by meditating and praying daily for the spread of Christ's kingdom; to study the Holy Scriptures regularly and the teachings of the Church; and, to make continuous efforts in service to bring others to Christ. More than likely, the most important fact to remember is that we are not fully functional unless we are connected or wired to God. This is how God created us in His image to glorify and praise Him in all that we do and with all that we have. This is our sole purpose in life as God created and programmed us to do. It is that simple.

There is no question that the modern Christian Church has been metamorphic over the thousands of years since its ancient beginnings. But to what degree and how far is in question. Many scholars think it has gone too far in the direction of secular humanism and adapted to the worlds standards. Like the pendulum, it needs to return to a more traditional structure and foundation that is only found in the lessons and practices of sacred theism. *The Pentagon of Faith Sacred Theism vs. Secular Humanism A Christian's Need for the Traditional Faith of our Fathers* is written to give the reader the necessary tools to strengthen us in a way that we may depart from sin and live as God intended us to live. We have spent decades in a metamorphic state that has led us to the brink of a moral, ethical and financial collapse. If we do not turn around, we may find ourselves falling off the brink and into a morass[251] that we will never be able to dig ourselves out of or overcome. So you think it might not happen, don't laugh, it happened to Sodom and Gomorrah.[252]

We are often led astray by our desires to have our cake and eat it too as the old saying goes. But, let's be more specific; the 'free love' seeds of secular humanism of the sixties was no less a temptation than the 'apple' in the Garden of Eden. The seeds of free love are a temptation that has just as severe a consequence as original sin. It seems that on

---

[251] Morass. (2001). Random House College Dictionary. *Random House Webster's College Dictionary 2nd Revised and Updated.* Random House, Inc. New York, New York. www.randomhouse.com. Page 562.

[252] Holy Bible, The. (2004). The Holy Bible. *The Holy Bible Authorized King James Version.* World Publishing. Nashville, Tennessee. www.worldpublishing.com. The Old Testament. Moses. The Book of Genesis 19:1-29. Pages 8-9.

the basis of 'love' we have opened the door to that proverbial Trojan horse who has entered our fortress with all the false promises and delusions that caused us to change or modify our ancient doctrines and traditions. Love is not lust. Love is not free. Love comes with a price. And that price was the blood on the Cross at Calvary. Love requires commitment and discipline. Love is of God and is God.

Love overcomes a multitude of sins. No doubt we should love our enemies as the Scripture says. No doubt we are commanded to love our neighbor as ourselves. An unbridled love is not a license to sin. In the attitude reflecting free love, Christianity felt the need to change our traditional practices and subsequently we have become an all inclusive and tolerant religion. Resistance to change meant we were out of touch, or intolerant, or prejudice, or chauvinist, or old fashioned, or too rigid, or hate-filled, or racist according to the proponents of secular humanism. It seems the enemies of sacred theism like to call names to disrupt us. Love means a disciplined commitment from a benevolent Heavenly Father whose love is unconditional. God does love us but He does not love our sin. We have to be separate from sin before God can welcome us into His arms. Don't think God is not without prejudice. He is prejudiced. In God's eyes, we accept His Son Jesus Christ and go to heaven, or we reject His Son and go to hell.

God is not tolerant. He does not tolerate sin. A man who is tolerant is a man who stands for nothing and everything including all Gods. An intolerant man is principled and lives by a set of values that keeps him in check so that he does not fall into temptation and sin. Therefore, I recommend that you seek the sacred theism way of life and depart from the life of secular humanism that has so thoroughly permeated our society and world. If we return to the traditional faith of our fathers, then we will return the pendulum of destruction and separation from God into the pendulum of salvation and presence with the Lord Jesus Christ.

I wanted to close with an article written as an omen by Rabbi Daniel Lapin[253]. He shares the title of America's Rabbi

---

[253] Lapin, Rabbi Daniel. (2006) Internet article. www.rabbidanielllapin.com.

with Rabbi Shumley and Rabbi Spero. The article addresses the dire circumstances where we as Christians have found ourselves; and the potential devastation on the horizon if we do not return to a Godly life of sacred theism. Since we have been lured into complacency and our faith and conviction diluted by secular humanism, we face becoming future slaves to the forces of evil. This wakeup call is as follows:

> *"...There is no better term than propaganda blitzkrieg to describe what has been unleashed against Christian conservatives... Consider the long list of anti-Christian books that have been published in recent months. (Author's note: This was written in 2006 and there have been many more anti-Christian books printed since) Here are just a few samples of more than 30 titles, all from mainstream publishers: 'America Fascists: The Christian Right and the War on America', 'The Baptizing of America: The Religious Right's Plans for the Rest of Us', 'Religion Gone Bad: The Hidden Dangers of the Christian Right', 'Piety and Politics: The Right-wing Assault on Religious Freedom', 'The End of Faith: Religion, Terror, and the Future of Reason', 'Atheist Universe: The Thinking Person's Answer to Christian Fundamentalism'. What is truly alarming is that there are more of these books for sale at your local bookstore warning against the perils of fervent Christianity than those warning against the perils of fervent Islam. Does anyone seriously thing America is more seriously jeopardized by Christian conservatives that by Islamic zealots? I fear that many Americans believe just that in the same way many preWWII Westerners considered Churchill a bigger threat than Hitler... It is not just books but popular entertainment also that*

beams the most lurid anti-Christian propaganda into the hearts and minds of viewers. One need only think of who the real targets of the recent hit movie "Borat" are. The brilliant Jewish moviemaker Sacha Baron Cohen, as his title character using borderline dishonest wiles, lures some innocent but unsophisticated country folk, obviously Christians, to join him in his outrageously anti-Semitic antics. Cohen then triumphantly claims to have exposed anti-Semitism. In fact, he has revealed nothing other than the latent anti-Christianism of America's social, economic and academic secular elites. Even the recent PBS documentary, 'Anti-Semitism in the 21st Century: The Resurgence', managed to do more attacking Christianity than defending Judaism.

Richard Dawkins, an Oxford University professor, is one of the generals in the anti-Christian army of the secular left. American academia treats him with reverence and hangs on his every word when he insists that 'religious myths ought not to be tolerated.' For those with a slightly more tolerant outlook, he asks, "It's one thing to say people should be free to believe whatever they like, but should they be free to impose their beliefs on their children?' He suggests that the state should intervene to protect children from their parent's religious beliefs. Needless to say, he means Christian beliefs, of course. Muslim beliefs add to England's charmingly diverse cultural landscape.

The war is against those who regard the Bible to be God's revelation to humanity and the Ten Commandments to be His set of rules for all time. Phase one in this war is to make

> *Christianity, well, sort of socially unacceptable. Something only foolish, poor, and ugly people could turn to... Considerably more intellectual energy is being pumped into the propaganda campaign against Christianity that was ever delivered to the anti-smoking or anti-drunk driving campaigns. Fervent zealots of secularism are flinging themselves in the anti-Christian war with enormous fanaticism. If they succeed, Christianity will be driven underground, and its benign influence on the character of America will be lost. In its place will be a sinister secularism that menaces Bible believers of all faith. Once the voice of the Bible has been silenced, the war of Western Civilization can begin and we shall see a long night of barbarism descend on the West. Without a vibrant and vital Christianity, America is doomed, and without American the West is doomed. Which is why I, and Orthodox Jewish Rabbi, devoted to Jewish survival, the Torah and Israel am so terrified of American Christianity caving in. Most of us Jews are ready to stand with you. But you must lead. You must replace your timidity with nerve and your diffidence with daring and determination. You are under attack. Now is the tie to resist it.'*

These sobering words by Rabbi Lapin could very well come true for history tells us that Churchill was right when he sounded the alarm preceding WWII. Noah was right when he built the Ark. If this clarion call is not heeded, then we should be ready for a future that will be without parallel of the hardships a Christian will face. Fight the good fight; run the good race against secular humanism and impart the practices of sacred theism and *The Pentagon of Faith* into your everyday life. Prepare yourself for the challenging days ahead with the lessons and tools that are provided herein. It will help you and your families defend itself against the enemy. If the peril does not ensue, then we will be stronger Christians for applying these foundations found in this book. And you will reap a happier and more rewarding life ahead. If the peril does occur, then we will have the tools to engage successfully with the enemy and protect ourselves and our family, friends and neighbors.

In conclusion, St. Augustine wrote, 'Thou hast made us for thyself, and the heart of man is restless until it finds its rest in Thee.'[254] America is the richest and most secular and materialist country in the world, and we have the most unhappy and despairing people who take more antidepressants than any other culture or nation. Secular humanism and materialism will not bring happiness. Happiness, peace and joy are fruits of the Holy Spirit of God and of a life lived by the values of sacred theism. As I wrote earlier, St. Paul tells us that our flesh is at war with our spirit. So, if we seek the flesh of secular humanism rather than the spirit of sacred theism, then we will never be happy or at rest. Therefore, seek the inner sanctum of your being where your soul meets God. Get wired to God and stay connected. Repent and ask Jesus Christ to be Lord over your life. There, in that inner sanctum, you will find the peace and joy that passes all understanding. And your life will have a light that shines on the riches you posses which only come from heaven and our Heavenly Father. These are gifts and fruits that no earthly gift can compare. And heaven will shower you with many blessings from God. Thanks be to God.

---

[254] Encyclopedia of Religious Quotations, The. (1966). The Encyclopedia of Religious Quotations. *The Encyclopedia of Religious Quotations The definitive compendium of usable religious quotations from every source, every faith, every shade of opinion The indispensable reference work for speakers, clergymen, students, libraries Unique Authoritative.* Edited and Compiled by Frank S. Mead.
Fleming H. Revel Company. Westwood, New Jersey. Page 165.

Bibliography

1. Allison, Gregg R., *Historical Theology An Introduction to Christian Doctrine. A Companion to Wayne Grudem's Systematic Theology.* Zondervan Publications. Grand Rapids, Michigan. 2011.
2. Appleton, George. General Editor. *The Oxford Book of Prayer.* Oxford University Press. New York, New York. 1985.
3. Arnaz, Dezi and Lewis, Elliott. *The I Love Lucy Show.* Desilu Studios. Culver City, California. Columbia Broadcasting System Network. 1962-1968.
4. Barker, Kenneth L., *The NIV Study Bible New International Version.* Published by Zondervan. Biblica US, Inc. Grand Rapids, Michigan. 2011.
5. Barker, Kenneth L. and Kohlenberger, III, John R. *The Expositor's Bible Commentary Abridged Edition: Old Testament.* Zondervan. Grand Rapids, Michigan. 1994.
6. Barker, Kenneth L. and Kohlenberger, III, John R. *The Expositor's Bible Commentary Abridged Edition: New Testament.* Zondervan. Grand Rapids, Michigan. 1994.
7. Bess, Douglas. *Divided We Stand - A History of the Continuing Anglican Movement.* Apocryphile Press. Berkeley, California. 2002.
8. Bethune-Baker, James Franklin. *The Faith of the Apostles' Creed.* Abridged and Edited by W. Norman Pittenger. The Seabury Press. Greenwich, Connecticut. 1955.
9. Bettenson, Henry. Editor. *Documents of the Church.* Oxford University Press. New York, New York. 1960.
10. Bloom, Archbishop Anthony. *Living Prayer.* Templegate Publishers. Springfield, Illinois. 1966.

11. Boel, Cornelius. *The Holy Bible 1611 Edition King James Version.* Hendrickson Publishers, Inc. Peabody, Massachusetts. 2005.
12. Borg, Marcus, *Meeting Jesus for the First Time – The Historical Jesus & The Heart of Contemporary Faith.* Harper Publishers. San Francisco, California. A Division of Harper Collins Publishers. New York, New York. 1995.
13. Borsch, Frederick Houk. Editor. *Anglicanism and the Bible.* Morehouse-Barlow Company, Inc. Wilton, Connecticut. 1984.
14. Burt, Donald X. *Day by Day with Saint Augustine.* Liturgical Press. Collegeville, Minnesota. 2006.
15. Buttrick, George Arthur. *The Interpreter's Bible The Holy Scriptures in the King James and Revised Standard Versions with General Articles and Introduction, Exegesis, Exposition for Each Book of the Bible in Twelve Volumes.* Abington Press. Nashville, Tennessee. 1952.
16. Cabal, Ted. *The Apologetics Study Bible New English Standard Version Understand Why You Believe.* Holman Bible Publishers. Nashville, Tennessee. 2007.
17. Cantor, Norman F. *Medieval History Second Edition.* The MacMillan Company. Collier-MacMillan Canada, Ltd. Toronto, Ontario. 1963.
18. Chadwick, Henry. *The Early Church.* Pelican Books, Ltd. Harmondsworth, Middlesex, England. 1967.
19. Chadwick, Owen. *The Reformation.* Pelican Books, Ltd. Harmondsworth, Middlesex, England. 1964.
20. Childress, James F. and Macquarrie, John. *The Westminster Dictionary of Christian Ethics.* The Westminster Press. Philadelphia, Pennsylvania. 1967.
21. Church, Rev. Leslie F. *Matthew Henry's Commentary in One Volume Zondervan Classic Reference Series.* Marshall, Morgan & Scott, Ltd. Zondervan Publishers. Grand Rapids, Michigan. 1961.
22. Clinton, Dr. Tim and Straub, Dr., *God Attachment: Why You Believe, Act, and Feel The Way You Do About God.*

Howard Books. A Division of Simon & Shuster, Inc. New York, New York. 2010.

23. Cranmer, Thomas. *A Defense of the True and Catholic Doctrine of The Sacrament of the Body and Blood of Our Savior Christ, with a Confutation of Sundry Errors Concerning the Same Grounded and Established Upon God's Holy Word, And Approved by the Consent of the Most Ancient Doctors of the Church.* Published by Focus Christian Ministries Trust. Lewes, East Sussex, England. 1987.

24. Cranmer, Thomas. *The Homilies Appointed to be Read in Churches.* The Preservation Press of the Prayer Book Society USA. Savannah, Georgia. 2006.

25. Cranmer, Thomas. *The Book of Common Prayer and Administration of the Sacraments and Other Rites and Ceremonies of the Church, According to the Use of the Protestant Episcopal Church in the United States of America, Together with The Psalter of Psalms of David.* New York, New York. Oxford University Press. 1928.

26. Criswell, Dr. W.A, *The Believer's Study Bible New King James Version.* Thomas Nelson Publishers. Nashville, Tennessee. 1991.

27. Cruse, C. F., *Eusebius' Ecclesiastical History Complete and Unabridged New Updated Edition.* Hendrickson Publishers. Peabody, Massachusetts. 2011.

28. Della-Cioppa, Guy. *The Red Skelton Hour.* Desilu Productions. CBS Television City. Hollywood, California. National Broadcasting System Network and Columbia Broadcasting System Network. 1951-1971.

29. Dennis, Dr. Lane T., *The English Standard Version Study Bible.* Crossway Bibles. A publishing ministry of Good News Publishers. Wheaton, Illinois. 2008.

30. Dickens, A.G. *The English Reformation.* Schocken Books. New York, New York. 1969.

31. Dillenberger, John. *Martin Luther Selections from His Writings.* Anchor Books, Doubleday and Company, Inc., New York, New York. 1961.

32. Dix, Dom Gregory. *The Shape of Liturgy.* Robert MacLehose and Company, Ltd. The University Press. Glascow, Scotland. 1945.
33. Elmen, Paul. Editor. *The Anglican Moral Choice.* MorehouseBarlow Company, Inc. Wilton, Connecticut. 1983.
34. Forbush, Dr. William Byron, *Foxe's Book of Martyrs A History of the Loves, Sufferings, and Triumphant Deaths of the Early Christian and Protestant Martyrs.* Faithpoint Press. Produced by Cliff Roads Books. 2006.
35. Freemantle, Anne. *The Age of Belief - The Medieval Philosophers.* A mentor Book Published by The New American Library. New York, New York. 1954.
36. Geisler, Norman L. *Systematic Theology in One Volume Bible, God, Creation, Sin, Salvation, Church, Last Times.* Bethany House, Inc. Minneapolis, Minnesota. 2011.
37. Godwin, Johnnie and Edgemon, Roy Editors-in-Chief, *The Disciples Study Bible New International Version.* Holman Bible Publishers. A Cornerstone Bible. Nashville, Tennessee. 1988.
38. Gore, Charles. *The Body of Christ The Enquiry into the Institution and Doctrine of Holy Communion.* Charles Scribner's Sons. New York, New York. 1901.
39. Gresham, J. Wilmer. *The Beatitudes of Jesus Vesper Addresses on The Octave of Blessedness.* Melvin & Murgotten, Inc. San Jose, California. 1908.
40. Haykin, Michael A.G. *Rediscovering the Church Fathers Who They Were and How They Shaped The Church.* Crossway Publishers. Wheaton, Illinois. 2011.
41. Herman, Nicholas. *The Practice of the Presence of God: Conversations and letters of Nicholas Herman of Larraine, Brother Lawrence.* Christian Books Today, Ltd. Chorley, Lancashire, United Kingdom. 2009.
42. Hillerbrand, Hans J. Editor. *The Protestant Reformation.* Harper & Row Publishers, Inc. New York, New York. 1969.

43. Hutton, R.G., *The Divine Service of Praise and Prayer Throughout the Christian Year. Abridged Edition.* Lulu Publishers. Raleigh, North Carolina. Based on the Daily Service Book.1874.
44. James J., O'Donnell, *Augustine A New Biography.* Harper Collins Publishers. New York, New York. 2005.
45. James, M.R. Editor. *The New Testament Apocrypha (The definitive critical edition for over seventy years).* Apocryphile Press. Berkeley, California. 2004.
46. Johnson, Paul, *Synoptic Gospels A History of Christianity.* A Touchstone Book. Published by Simon & Shuster, Inc. Border Books. New York, New York. 1976.
47. Jones, Alexander. General Editor. *The Jerusalem Bible.* Doubleday & Company, Inc. Garden City, New York. 1966.
48. Jones, Tony. *The Sacred Way Spiritual Practices for Everyday Life.* Zondervan Press. Grand Rapids, Michigan. 2005.
49. Kaufman, Joanne. People Magazine. *The Fall of Jimmy Swaggart.* A Division of Time-Warner Publications. March 7, 1988. Vol. 29, No. 9.
50. Kelly, Mrs. Walt and Crouch, Jr., Bill, *The Best of Pogo.* A Fireside Book. Simon & Shuster Publishers. New York, New York. 1982.
51. Kerr, Hugh T., Editor. *A Compend of Luther's Theology.* The Westminster Press Publishers. Philadelphia, Pennsylvania. 1966.
52. Kohlenberger III, John R., *Today's Parallel Bible NIV NASB Updated KJV NLT.* The Zondervan Corporation. Zondervan Publishing House. Grand Rapids, Michigan. 2000.
53. Leonard, Sheldon. *The Dick Van Dyke Show.* Producers Carl Reiner, Bill Persky, Sam Denoff. Columbia Broadcasting System Network. Hollywood, California. 1961-1966.
54. Lowry, Charles W., *The First Theologians.* Gateway Editions. Chicago, Illinois. 1986.

55. Luther, Martin. *A Commentary on St. Paul's Epistle to the Galatians. A revised and completed translation based on the Middleton. Text.* Edited by Philip S. Watson. James Clarke & Company, Ltd., London, England. 1961.
56. MacCulloch, Diarmaid, *Christianity: The First Three Thousand Years.* Viking Books. Published by Penguin Group (USA), Inc. New York, New York. 2010.
57. MacArthur, Dr. John, *The MacArthur Study Bible English Standard Version.* Crossway Bibles. A publishing ministry of Good News Publishers. Wheaton, Illinois. 2010.
58. MacDonald, William. *The Believer's Bible Commentary. A Complete Commentary in One Volume New King James Bible Version.* Thomas Nelson Publishers, Inc. Nashville, Tennessee. 1995.
59. McKim, Donald K., *Westminster Dictionary of Theological Terms.* Westminster John Know Press. Louisville, Kentucky. 1996.
60. McReynolds, Paul R. *Word Study Greek-English New Testament with Complete Concordance.* Tyndale House Publishers, Inc. Carol Stream, Illinois. 1999.
61. Mead, Frank S., *The Encyclopedia of Religious Quotations.* Fleming H. Revell Company. Westwood, New Jersey. 1966.
62. Metzger, Bruce M. *An Introduction to the Apocrypha.* Oxford University Press. New York, New York. 1957.
63. Morton, Donna Hobeika, *Our Jewish Heritage.* Our Jewish Heritage Endorsed by Sid Roth. 2011.
64. Mounce, Dr. William D., *The Basics of Biblical Greek Grammar.* Zondervan Publishing House. Grand Rapids, Michigan. 1999.
65. Neill, Stephen. *Anglicanism* Pelican Books, Ltd. Harmondsworth, Middlesex, England. 1965.
66. Niebuhr, Richard H. *The Purpose of the Church and Its Ministry.* Harper & Brothers, New York, New York. 1956.
67. O'Donnell, James. *Augustine A New Biography.* Harper Collins Publishers. New York, New York. 2005.

68. O'Loughlin, Thomas. *The Didache A Window on the Earliest Christians.* Baker Academic. A Division of Baker Publishing Group. Grand Rapids, Michigan. 2010.
69. Paul II, John. *Second Edition Catechism of the Catholic Church Revised in Accordance with the Official Latin Text.* Promulgated By Pope John Paul II. Published by Doubleday. A Division of Random House, Inc. New York, New York. 1995.
70. Proctor, Francis and Frere, Walter Howard. *A New History of the Book of Common Prayer with a Rationale of Its Offices.* MacMillan and Company, Limited. London, England. 1908.
71. Reuben, Aaron and Ross, Bob. *The Andy Griffith Show.* Desilu Studios. Columbia Broadcasting System Network. Culver City, California. 1960-1968.
72. *Season of Reflection The NIV Bible in 365 Daily Readings with Special Helps on Prayer.* Published by the International Bible Society. Colorado Springs, Colorado. 1984.
73. Schaff, David and Schaff, Philip. *The Creeds of Christendom With a History and Critical Notes Volume I The History of Creeds.* Baker Books. A Division of Baker Book House Company. Grand Rapids, Michigan. 2007.
74. Schaff, Phillip. *History of the Christian Church. History of the Christian Church Volume I Apostolic Christianity from the Birth of Christ to the Death of St. John.* Hendrickson Publishers. Peabody, Massachusetts. 2011.
75. Senior, Donald, *The Catholic Study Bible New American Bible.* Oxford University Press, Inc. New York, New York. 1990.
76. Shelley, Bruce L., *Church History in Plain Language. Updated 2nd Edition Church History in Plain Language.* Thomas Nelson Publishers. Nashville, Tennessee. 1995.
77. Shepherd, Jr. Massey Hamilton. *The Oxford American Prayer Book Commentary.* Oxford University Press. New York, New York. 1963.

78. Sparks, Dr. Jack Norman. *The Orthodox Study Bible New King James Version*. St. Athanasius Academy Septuagint. Thomas Nelson Publishers. Thomas Nelson, Inc. Nashville, Tennessee. 2008.
79. Staniforth, Maxwell. Translator. *Early Christian Writings The Apostolic Fathers*. Dorset Press. New York, New York. 1968.
80. St. Augustine of Hippo. *The City of God*. Edited by David Knowles. Pelican Books Ltd. Harmondsworth, Middlesex, England. 1972.
81. St. Augustine of Hippo. *The Confessions of St. Augustine*. Translated by Edward B. Pusey. Collier Books. New York, New York. 1961.
82. Streeter, B.H. *The Primitive Church*. The MacMillan Company, Inc. New York, New York. 1929.
83. *The Anglican Breviary*. Frank Gavin Liturgical Foundation, Inc. The Lakeside Press. 1998.
84. *The Holy Bible Authorized King James Version*. World Publishing. Nashville, Tennessee. 2004.
85. Thompson, Dr. Frank Charles, *The Thompson Chain-Reference Bible King James Version*. B.B. Kirkbride Bible Company, Inc. Indianapolis, Indiana. 2007.
86. Tyndale, William and Coverdale, Myles. *The 1599 Geneva Bible Patriot's Edition The Holy Scriptures Contained in the Old and New Testaments*. Tolle Lege Press. White Hall Press. White Hall, West Virginia. 2010.
87. Vogel, Arthur A. Editor. *Theology in Anglicanism*. MorehouseBarlow. Wilton, Connecticut. 1984.
88. Ward, Benedicta. *The Sayings of the Desert Fathers*. Cistercian Publications. Trappist, Kentucky. 1975
89. White, William. *Lectures on the Catechism of the Protestant Episcopal Church with Supplementary Lectures; One on the Ministry, the other on the Public Service and Books on Select Subjects in the Lectures*. Philadelphia, Pennsylvania. 1813.

90. Wolf, William. *Anglican Spirituality*. Morehouse-Barlow Company, Inc. Wilton, Connecticut. 1982.
91. Zizioulas, John D. *Eucharist Bishop Church – The Unity of the Church in the Divine Eucharist and the Bishop during the First Three Centuries*. Translated by Elizabeth Theokritoff. Holy Cross Orthodox Press. Brookline, Massachusetts. 2001.

www.ingramcontent.com/pod-product-compliance
Lightning Source LLC
LaVergne TN
LVHW021703060526
838200LV00050B/2488